INDESCRIBABLE

CANDICE DERMAN

QUARTET

To my husband, protector of my secret life and my joy in everything else. I love you.

Indescribable
adjective
too unusual, extreme, or indefinite to be adequately described.

eight

My name is Candice Derman. I am eight years old and I live in Johannesburg, South Africa. Yesterday I kissed my girlfriend like I was a boy. My tongue went into her mouth. It felt wet. Naughty. Nice. Wrong.

I like swimming parties, spare ribs and cats. My mom got divorced. My father moved out but I'm not sad. He was always cross and slept a lot. My mom's getting remarried. I am so excited about my new dad. He gives me so much attention. The attention feels good when he's not touching me there. I am eight. I love my sisters, playing and puppies. I know it's wrong what he is doing. Tomorrow he will stop. I know it.

***

My mom, dad, four sisters and I are on holiday in Durban. Mom and I go for a walk on the beach. She is so beautiful with long dark hair and blue eyes. I'm so happy, just my mom and me. The sea goes on forever; I'm not sure where it ends and the sky begins. I love this moment, this life. I like being eight. I want to stay eight forever.

I see a man sitting on a towel. He's wearing a black Speedo swimming costume. He is tall, big, a little handsome and a little overweight. My mom stops to talk to him. I notice a slight touch of hands between them. They know each other and like each other. He makes her laugh. Her head goes back and her mouth opens. I see her perfect teeth, her tongue and the back of her throat. I like my mom like this – happy and laughing. She sits down next to him and I sit in between them. I'm being naughty and feel frustrated. They're enjoying each other and not really taking much notice of me. Eventually they do.

'What's your name?'

'Candice. What's yours?'

'Joe.' He smiles at me.

'Want an ice cream?' he asks.

'No thanks.'

'Come on, have one!'

I like this attention. 'Okay, chocolate.'

And so off we go to find ice cream.

It is on this day on the beach, with the two people who will become my biggest influences growing up, that Joe and I begin our father-daughter relationship.

'I need to wee,' I announce.

'I'll take you,' Joe says.

'Ma, you take me.'

I don't want Joe to take me: this is girl business.

'Let Joe take you.'

'But Ma …'

There is a self-consciousness about me already: I feel awkward but I say yes. He can wait outside for me and be my bodyguard.

Joe takes me off to find a loo. We don't.

'Go behind the bush.'

'No, people will see me.'

'Come on, I'll make sure no one comes.'

'Okay.' Bodyguards are handy.

I pull down my bikini bottoms and wee as quickly as possible. Joe smiles over at me, I smile at Joe. I like him. He got me an ice cream, took me to wee and has made my mom's eyes glossy, more than what most dads do. I pull up my bikini bottoms and we walk hand in hand back to my mom, back to the towel. His hand is so big that my hand gets comfortably swallowed in his. I sit between them again, content. I fall asleep.

It's evening and I am with my dad and sisters in our beach hotel. My body feels bad. I don't understand this feeling. I feel guilty because I had fun with Joe and I wish he were my dad. I feel guilty because I think my mom wishes Joe were her husband. Mom is tanned and beautiful and dressed to kill, with tight stonewashed jeans, big hoop earrings and shiny pink lipstick. Her top exposes one shoulder, showing off her bronzed skin; the other shoulder is covered, hiding her skin but her eyes are still shining with a secret love.

My sisters are upset. They don't know where we were all day and are jealous because they wanted to be part of the fun. My dad is cross.

'Where were you two?' he asks me, the two lines between his eyes getting deeper as he talks to us.

'Walking on the beach.'

'Who with?'

'No one,' I lie, my first real lie. I must protect my mom.

Mom doesn't seem bothered. 'We just lost track of time. We had ice creams and lay in the sun.' She speaks in half-truths.

Dad walks away: he knows something but we've said nothing. I start playing with my toys and the badness melts away. I am eight, I love dolls, putting on concerts with my sisters, and attention. It's summer, we're right by the sea, how bad can life be?

The drive back home to Johannesburg in the Kombi is long, but I like it. My sisters and I sit snugly, side-by-side, row-by-row, chattering all the way. Dad and Mom aren't talking and our chatter makes their silence seem even louder.

The holiday is over, our tans fade and we are not sure what is going on with our parents. School starts, Dad goes back to work and Mom carries on being the greatest mom in the world. On weekends Dad sleeps or runs and Mom shops or takes us on picnics. Dad is strict and stern and Mom is outgoing and loving. His hair is getting greyer and thinner and hers is growing fuller and longer. Mom's smile is wide and toothy and Dad stops smiling.

My dad, sisters and I are around our breakfast table, and I'm tucking into my egg-in-the-middle toast.

EIGHT

'Your mother and I love you all very much,' Dad announces.

My sisters and I sit quietly, watching our grey father speak.

'I'm moving out.'

We are silent. I try to swallow quietly.

Mom comes flying into the room. She has just been for her morning run and is glowing with beauty and perspiration. The sun told her he was in love with her and she believed him. Mom sweeps past all of us, leaving her glow behind.

Dad packs his bags and takes his broken heart with him.

Our lives are changing; I'm excited about the new. My mom, sisters and I are going to play full time, or at least when I get back from school.

I am so scared, scared of the dark. It's three in the morning and I've had a bad dream. I often have bad dreams and hear old women cackling. I can't be alone in my room so I often sneak into my mom's bed when she is sleeping. Tonight Joe is sleeping over. I tiptoe into my mom's room, making sure I don't wake her and Joe. It's so dark I can't see a thing, and I touch the walls as I try to find the bed. The darkness fills up my body and all I can hear is my beating heart. I'm worried: I don't want my mom to be cross. I'm a big girl and shouldn't be sleeping in her bed, but I'm afraid. What if my nightmares come true and nasty things happen to me?

I slip quietly into the bed next to Joe, certain Mom won't notice. I'll be protected, my nightmares will become dreams and I'll ride on unicorns, eat candyfloss and have mermaids as friends.

Joe touches me down there. I hold my breath and move his thick hand away. The early morning is silent except for the sound of distant chanting coming from the church where the Indian people pray. I listen to my mom and Joe breathing. I hear my heart beating in my head. A few seconds later his hand comes back and I move it away. It comes back. I leave it. I hold my breath. It's the first time I've held my breath for longer than a minute. I'm more scared of this than the dark. Is this a nightmare? He starts to play with me. I didn't know a wee place was used in this way. I'm cold, I'm hot and I'm still. I'm paralysed.

In this moment I learn I can become an object. My body knows what to do without me telling it. It is in charge, I'm emptied out, I've disappeared. No longer a human being, I take on another form. I have no heart, organs, skin. I have transformed, I'm the bed, the mattress, and the foam inside the mattress. I'm not here, I'm there, I'm above me looking down, I'm nothing.

Morning arrives. I fell asleep before I could sneak out without my mom noticing. She wakes me up and she's angry.

'Go and get ready for school. I don't want you sleeping in my bed anymore, you are not a baby.'

'Okay.'

'Morning sweetheart,' Joe whispers.

'Morning,' heart beating, I'm human again.

Joe looks lovingly at me. 'Go on, you don't want to be late for school.' Perhaps he doesn't remember what happened.

Did something bad happen or not? I can't remember, but I can.

I'm a different girl from the one I was the day before. Something's changed. I'm the same but different. There was a space in my head that used to be filled with the Muppets and Strawberry Shortcake. They've moved out and left a vacant spot that darkness has taken over.

I am Candice Derman. I am eight years old. I go to Linksfield Primary School. My house is close to the school. It's a big house with many rooms. My mom's favourite room is the white room: it's only used for special occasions and maybe one day I'll get married there. Our garden is huge with old trees that look after us and a pool that is big enough for ten grown-ups to fit into. At the bottom of the garden there is a fishpond and a jungle gym. I often imagine fairies playing in the trees and fish talking to each other about their day. Most summer mornings, before school, my sisters and I jump into the pool. The water is always cool and crisp and gets us ready for our day.

My sister Romy and I walk to school together. She cups my neck with her hand and tells me a story:

7

'Once upon a time there were two sisters who loved each other very much ...' And with that introduction Romy and I jump on our magic carpet of imagination. As we walk, the tall jacaranda trees that line the road drop their purple flowers on the ground and it's a perfect setting for Romy's story. Growing up in Johannesburg is wonderful: it's like living in a colouring-in book that has already been coloured. Clear blue skies most days and green grass after the afternoon rains. I look up at the clouds passing above us in a slow lazy way. I wish Romy and I could lie in them. I imagine the clouds being cool and soft.

'To be continued,' says Romy, and off we go our separate ways.

I'm the school mascot. I do well in school. I can spell, make jokes and run. I'm happy, brave, naughty and nice. People tell me I'm pretty. I have blue eyes and short, curly, dark brown hair, and I'm the shortest girl in my class.

I am not really involved in school today; it is boring and I can still hear the chanting in my head. I'm reading aloud to the class, only I don't hear myself or see my friends. I'm here in my class, in my school uniform, but I'm not. I can't wait for break so I can run around the playground, play rough with the boys and swing on the swing. I'm here but I'm not.

My school day comes to an end. I'm happy but I'm not. Romy and I wait for Mom to pick us up. She's late. She's often late. She has three other daughters to fetch from school, and when you're the last two in line, it's to be expected.

My sisters and I squash into my mom's yellow Volkswagen Beetle, our tiny runabout. We sit in order of age: Karin in the front, Jodi and Kim in the back seat and Romy and I in the open boot.

'How was school?'

'Good.'

'What did you learn today?'

'Nothing.' Here I'm really telling the truth.

Jodi hands Romy and me a burger. Everyone's getting stuck in.

The car smells of tomato sauce, onions, meat and Mommy's perfume. This makes me so happy. I forget the badness that has invaded my body. I am full, excited and ready for all that life throws at me.

Being part of a big family is fun. I like being the youngest in a crowd of girls. The problem is that now my mom and dad aren't together anymore, we will no longer live as five girls in one house, and that spoils everything. Mom has told us that we are not allowed to sit on the fence and have to make a choice. Either we are with my dad or with my mom, no in-between. Of course I've chosen my mom. Romy and Jodi have chosen my dad. When they move out my mom thinks they don't love her and closes her heart to them for a while.

Karin is my oldest sister. She is eighteen. She has dark round eyes, curly hair and a chubby body. She is moving to Israel. I think she wants adventure in her life, or maybe she just wants to run away. She is going to live on a kibbutz. Mom tells me it's a place where people work and live together and that they share everything. I think it sounds terrible; I hate getting hand-me-down clothes from my sisters. Karin and I are not close: she doesn't play with me and she likes boys too much.

Jodi is the second oldest. She is a runner, tall, skinny, with the longest legs you ever did see. She is smart and gets good marks at school. Jodi is Dad's favourite; he is her running coach and they always watch Rocky together before a race. She loves our dog Lulu with all her heart even though she is small and yaps a lot. When she moved out to live with my dad she took Lulu with her. We don't have a relationship; she's too old, runs too much and is very serious.

Kim loves all things girly and pink is her favourite colour. She is a ballet dancer and has leg warmers in all different colours. She lives with my mom, Joe and me. Sometimes we talk and laugh. Sometimes we don't talk and just fight. Kim doesn't like that Mommy and I are so close. She thinks I'm spoilt because I'm the youngest and I always get what I want. Mom sometimes takes me shopping and hides the clothes away from Kim so as not to upset her.

And then there is Romy. She is the peacemaker of the family. She is kind and funny. She loves Michael Jackson more than anyone else in the world: I come a close second. She also loves to run. I tell myself that's why she goes to live with Jodi, Lulu and my dad.

EIGHT

Romy is three years and a bit older than me. She seems a lot older. I used to watch Romy's every move. She's good at everything she does. I love her. Everybody loves Romy; she's too 'all things nice' not to. When she moves out she leaves me with her doll's house, the dolls that live in the house and the farm animals. I don't want the house, the dolls or the animals. I want Romy but she has gone. Her bags are packed and my heart is broken.

We are scattered, no more a kibbutz of a family. I see my sisters less and less, except for Kim, but all their roles in my life are small. Mom and Joe are my main attraction.

I've joined the Cubs. Only boys are meant to go but a few of my girlfriends and I have become members. It is such fun. I love Cubs: all the activity, the khaki shorts and top, and the boys. I go on Saturday mornings. We swim, learn how to tie knots and learn about plants and animals. I love the Cub leader. He is kind and fun. Joe doesn't like him much. I'm starting to realise Joe doesn't like a lot of the people I like. This makes me confused but I also don't really care. I'm hoping Cubs will teach me to be one of the boys and to be strong, and I'm hoping it stops the nightmares and the badness that enters my body.

'You have to stop going to Cubs,' Mom announces.
'Why?'
'You're not a boy. Some of the parents aren't happy

11

that a few girls have joined.'

'But who cares?'

'Candice, they don't want you to go anymore. Stop asking questions and let it go.'

'But I love it. Please, please let me go.'

'No, enough. I'm sorry, Candice, there is nothing I can do.'

I am so upset that I have to stop going. So upset because I have only been part of the team for a short while and I'm not tough or strong yet and I'm still having nightmares and Joe's still touching me in my privates and I don't have any badges yet.

Joe wears his Father Christmas red jersey a lot and drives around in his old white Mercedes Benz. His brown hair is untidy and that makes his handsomeness less. This isn't working for Mom and she starts styling Joe. He gets a haircut, new shirts, jeans, suits, and some fancy shoes. Mom gets him a new car and a new diet, so his belly can go down. Joe's feeling good; he is all puffed up and happy. Mom smiles at her accomplishment.

I love Joe. Joe loves me. We play a lot, he puts me on his shoulders, swings me around, comes swimming with me and lets me eat sweets. I was being silly to think that I needed a Cub leader in my life: Joe is my Cub leader. He teaches me about things I didn't know and gives me the guidance to help me grow.

I'm excited about Joe and Mommy getting married; he's going to be my new dad. I can't wait. In the day he is very, very good and I try to forget about the night, when he is very, very bad. After the wedding he'll stop because I'll be his daughter. From this moment on I refer to Joe as Dad and my real dad as Lionel. That's just what happened, I had no choice.

My new dad tells me he always wanted a daughter and I am the perfect one. He tells me I'm smart, funny and talented. I tell him he's the best, the best father in the world. We have connected and I'm excited. I've never felt this before. I don't think my real dad loved me but my new dad does. I can feel it all the time, lucky me, lucky eight-year-old me.

Between the love his fingers find their way inside my body. I'm sitting at my dressing table. He begins to touch me there. He goes inside me. I'm sore, it's sore. I become the chair, the wood, the fabric and then I become nothing. In these moments, I know my nightmares are real, I know I'm bad and that G-d doesn't love me. I know it's wrong. His fingers are in my insides but I can't stop him. I'm frozen and afraid, I don't recognise him or me. I wish I were a boy; I want to go back to the Cubs. I'm lost and scared, I can't breathe. He leaves my bedroom and takes his fingers with him. Mom comes to kiss me goodnight.

'I love you.'

'I know.'

'Isn't Joe perfect?'

'Yes.'

'He's going to be the best dad, isn't he? We're going to be happy, aren't we?'

'Yes.'

My mom holds me a little too tight and tells me she loves me. I know her piercing blue eyes are full of hope. She is always full of hope, and likes to believe she can fill a room with an Alice in Wonderland magic. Most of the time she can, but not tonight.

'I love you, Ma.'

She leaves and I'm alone, more alone than ever. I find my own fingers walking down my tummy towards the place Dad touches. I begin to touch myself. It feels bad, it feels good, I feel bad, and I don't care. I fall asleep, have nightmares and wake up terrified. I can't stay in my room. I can't go into my mom's room. I'm stuck and I'm scared.

It's darker and more evil in my room than it is in my mom's bed so I sneak into the bedroom. Mom and Dad are sleeping and I slip into the bed next to Dad. I don't want my mom to be cross. I'm praying Dad doesn't wake up. He doesn't, but his fingers do and I begin to fly above myself, watching me, not recognising me. Dad touches, my body responds and I'm terrified. I hate myself.

I wake up before my mom and dad and quickly run to my bedroom and get dressed.

'Candice, breakfast.'

'Coming.'

'How did you sleep? You look tired, are you okay?'

'Mom, I'm fine.'

'You're perfect.'

'Thanks Mom.'

'Come on, eat up and let's go.'

I'm on my way to being an A-plus liar. I can hide all my fears and rise above the darkness, play with my friends, contribute in class and make silly jokes. Perfect little me.

My mom doesn't know I've already gone, left the house, my school and the playground. I'm with my unicorns, away, away from here, in my silent prison.

Dad kisses my forehead, he is being a father, strong, kind and caring. He places his hand on my shoulder.

'See you later sweetheart, enjoy school.'

'Thanks.'

I hug Dad. I hug him because he loves me and I like being loved. I hug him because I love him and I like loving. Maybe he keeps making mistakes and I need to forgive him; maybe my prison won't be so bad after all.

I'm an eight-year-old girl who loves bubblegum ice cream and milk suckers. My dad kisses me with his tongue and touches me in places that feel bad. I love my sisters, my friends and my mom. I love Cabbage Patch dolls and Barbie. Dad loves me. I know because he told me how special I am, how pretty, how G-d wants this to happen between us and that our love is so deep that only G-d can understand. That's why we must never tell people because they wouldn't understand this powerful love. I play his game, play with fear and anxiety. No one knows our game; no one knows I am starting to become crippled by fear, lies and loneliness.

There are other times in my life when there is no tongue, no touching and no fingers. I've learned how to have fun, learned how to be my age, learned how to kick back like the other eight-year-olds. So I'm normal, not so normal, this is my new kind of normal.

'Dad, I've been invited to a birthday party tomorrow. Please can I go?'

'But we've got plans for this weekend and I don't like you spending the day away.'

'Please, Dad.'

I've also learned that the only way I will be able to go to this party is if Dad, in broad daylight, in his office, can touch what I now call my fanny – thanks to Dad's teachings. If he can touch it in his way, and I can become nothing, become an object long enough, I can go to the party.

He begins. I become the sheet of paper, the pen, the desk, the wood, and then I become nothing.

'You can go.'

'Thanks, Dad.'

I pull up my panties. Yippee, I'm going to the party. A day away from here, from him, this man I love, this man I'm scared of. This man I call Dad.

When he isn't being a husband, a father, a businessman, a son, a smoker, he finds his tongue a new home, inside my fanny. First it is the tip of his tongue, an uncomfortable fly landing on my sensitivities. I want to slap it away, slap him away. But it becomes firmer, stronger and parts my private lips. No longer a fly, it becomes more demanding. My legs forced open, he pushes his rough tongue in her. I hate this, I hate her. I feel her opening, letting his tongue deeper inside me.

Things I learned at eight:

1. *Happiness comes and goes.*
2. *How to kiss with the tongue.*
3. *Sums.*
4. *Girls aren't allowed to go to Cubs.*
5. *A man's thing can go hard.*
6. *I'm pretty and can get attention.*
7. *I love to act and want to be famous.*
8. *I can leave my body and be nowhere.*
9. *I can keep secrets.*
10. *I know how to miss someone.*
11. *I know I can get on with life.*
12. *My body can become an object.*

nine

I'm no one; I'm the air, the desk, the floor and the carpet. We are lying on the floor; he's hard and sticky. I'm his toy, I'm invisible. I'm afraid and I hate myself. Does G-d hate me?

'Want to get some bubblegum ice cream?'

'Please,' I say with no expression.

I don't want bubblegum ice cream, I don't want to be here with him in his office, I don't want to be me, I don't want to exist. I pull up my panties. My legs are tired, my in-between place is sore. His knuckles are too large for that space. I feel sick. Maybe the ice cream will help.

We're in the car and he tells me how wonderful and special I am. I wonder if wonderful and special equals no one, nothing, invisible and dirty. Dad tells me G-d loves me, Dad says he loves me so much that he can't help himself. I'm thinking I must be very special to be so loved.

My ice cream is delicious. The bubblegum is hard and chewy, the ice cream cold, blue and soft. I lick it, love it. It soothes my insides as it slides down into my tummy; it feels like medicine and I feel healed.

'Good?' Dad asks.

'Better than good!'

It's my birthday. I've eaten ice cream and opened so many presents. I got the best stuff: jelly shoes and bracelets from Kim, a Hello Kitty purse from Gran, and pretty clothes from Mom and Dad. Mom, Gran and Kim tell me they love me and I again think I must be so very special to be so loved. G-d, Dad, Mom, Gran and Kim love me, Candice Derman. I'm so lucky.

For my ninth birthday I have a swimming party. I have lots of friends over. We swim, laugh, eat and play games. I love these moments, carefree and happy. My mom throws the best birthday parties. Sometimes she organises treasure hunts, sometimes she arranges ponies, and sometimes there are clowns. I love birthdays; I wish I could have one every day.

They are like forgiveness, G-d loves me again and he doesn't think I'm evil, bad and nasty. G-d thinks I'm his princess and I feel good, clean and beautiful. Everyone is celebrating me. There is so much chatting and laughing. Dad's being so nice to all my friends, he makes them giggle and scream as he runs after them in the garden. I love him now, all playful and kind. He looks at me and summons up a big smile.

'Happy birthday, my love.'

'Thanks, Dad.'

'One day you are going to be the most beautiful woman in the world.'

'Thanks, Dad.'

NINE

Happy birthday to me.
Hard.
Happy birthday to me.
Hard, hairy.
Happy birthday, dear Candice.
Small, sore, wet.
Happy birthday to me.
Squirt, sticky, smelly, warm.

There are a few things I want to be when I grow up:

1. *An actress.*
2. *A dog walker.*
3. *A mother.*
4. *A model.*

When I blow out the candles on my birthday cake, I close my eyes and make some wishes. Maybe one of them will come true some day.

My soon-to-be stepbrothers, John and Richard, are at the party. They live in Zimbabwe with their mother and stay over during their holidays. I like them, especially Richard. He reminds me of me: naughty, loud, fun and cross. The only difference between us is that everything he feels, everyone knows about. I'm hoping to be his girlfriend, even though I am his stepsister. I imagine he is a good kisser.

I'm nine, and I can blow bubblegum bubbles better than anyone else. My bubbles are massive and when they pop, they cover my nose and mouth. Usually I find this funny, but not today; today I can't breathe, I am sure I will suffocate and die. I start peeling the sticky goo from my face. Everyone is watching and laughing. I'm laughing too, a nervous laugh. I tell myself it's only sticky gum, Candice, not the sticky stuff that comes out of Dad. It tastes nice, not like Dad. Silly me for thinking I could die from gum. I wonder if I could die from 'cum'; that's what Dad calls it.

'Happy birthday, Candice!' everyone shouts.

I smile. I'm nine. I have cake, chocolate and sweets to eat and lots of presents to open. What have I got to be afraid of? Let the party go on and on.

The night of my birthday party I go to bed happy and full, my head spinning from sugar and treats. I wish I could put my ninth birthday in a snow globe and stay in this day forever. Everyone with their smiles plastered on their faces and Dad, just being Dad, protecting me from the snow.

The touching increases and things in the 'I-wish-Dad-wasn't-doing-this-to-me' department grow. His fat, pink tongue has found its way into my once smiling mouth. He smells like smoke: Dad is a big smoker. He wakes up in the morning and inhales, goes to sleep at night and exhales. The bed smells of cigarettes, his clothes smell of cigarettes, he smells of cigarettes.

The worst smell, though, is his mouth with its dragon-like tongue. The first time his tongue entered my mouth I wanted to vomit, a loud, convulsing never-ending vomit. His tongue felt big and for a few moments I forgot how to breathe through my nose. His tongue slapped my tongue and hit the back of my throat. I thought he was going to lick my insides out, suck my blood and steal my heart, but he didn't. When his tongue left my swollen mouth my insides were still intact, my blood was still pumping fast around my body, and I knew my heart was still there because it was beating so hard I thought it would thump me to death.

I was wrong; nothing happened. I continued to live and a new kind of normal took over.

On the morning of the wedding I have butterflies in my tummy. I'm so excited about the day, about my dress, about all the guests, but mostly I'm excited about Joe becoming my real dad.

The wedding is perfect. Everyone is so happy and filled with celebration. I recite a poem. I love the attention and feel on top of the world. Everyone laughs when they should, and claps when I finish, even though my poem has nothing to do with love or weddings. The best part of the wedding is seeing Romy. I haven't seen her in ages and I miss her so badly. My mom's so happy she is here and her heart has opened up once again.

Romy arrives in an ugly grey and yellow dress and here I am in my beautiful white and pink dress. I hate my dress, I hate that Romy is uncomfortable. I love her and I love that she came. Even though her dress is dull she looks prettier than anyone at the wedding. I'm so proud of Romy; what a perfect day.

I want to be loved, wear beautiful dresses, play with my friends and be protected by my parents. I don't want night-time to come. I don't want a wee place; I want to stitch it up and close it forever.

After the wedding, life goes back to some kind of normality. Dad's mom moves in with us, so now I have a new gran. She is old, fat and wrinkled with a mouth that turns down, and her hair is grey and falls to her waist. She plaits it and puts it in a bun. She loves her son, Jesus and G-d and I try to love her. Mom thinks she also needs a new style. Gran gets a short haircut, new shirts, blouses and fancy shoes. I notice her mouth slowly turning upwards.

I go to school, shop with Mom, play with my friends, fight with Kim, do my homework, and have nightmares. Romy stops coming around and Dad continues touching me. And he's getting hold of me more often during the day.

We have moved to an even bigger house, we are rich. We are rich because my mom's dad was rich, which made my gran, my mom and now my dad rich. It once made Lionel rich but when he left my grandfather's business and my mom, he became poor. My grandparents are now dead and Dad is running the furniture business.

Our house has many floors. We have a dining room, TV room, five bedrooms and a snooker room. Outside there is a jacuzzi, sauna, swimming pool, pond, tennis court, small gym and Dad's office.

We have three black people working for us, Anna, Lizzy and Lucas. They have worked for my mom for many years. Anna is like my second mom. She makes sure that I sparkle as clean as the house. She comes on holiday with us, dresses me up as a little Zulu girl, makes me pap and collects bottled seawater, though I don't know what she uses it for. Lizzy helps Anna clean and cook; she's my third mom. Lucas is our gardener. He takes care of everything growing and green. He has magic fingers and flowers bloom when he touches them.

We have two German shepherds called Sasha and Nero and two Persian cats called Tuppence and Smurf They all live together in harmony and are among my best friends. I'm living on my very own island called Villa Be Vardi, that's what Dad calls our kingdom. I'm not sure about what goes on outside our kingdom, I don't know who the President is, who our neighbours are or why there are no black children at my school.

I'm in our snooker room. It has a bar and behind the bar are tall stools. I'm on a stool, legs spread over the wooden seat. Dad often puts me in this position. The hard wood pushes into me and my lower back is so sore. In a way, I like the pain; in a way, it distracts me from what's really going on. I forget about my lower back banging into the back of the chair and I see Dad touching himself. I see his large, hard, hairy, ugly thing. He is moaning, his eyes have rolled back, he's not thinking of anything. It seems like Dad's not really there; he is but he isn't. This is not Dad, it is a monster.

His tongue has left my insides and his fingers are there instead. He's moving them in and out hard and fast; it is sore, and he doesn't care. He looks desperate and out of control. He starts to make loud noises. He takes his fingers away, loses his balance, opens his eyes and the white stuff spurts out of his wee place. The sticky goo flies out onto me and I smell the smell. It is strong. It's a smell I don't understand, a smell I don't like. Dad's coming back, I see him entering his body.

'Go and bath. Get cleaned up.'

'Okay.'

'I love you, you know that, don't you?'

'Yes.'

'I love you more than anything. You're the best daughter in the world.'

This is my new kind of normal.

I'm in the bath and I feel nothing, I am nothing. I am numb. I'm washing myself but can't feel myself doing it. I pull out the plug and let the water down the plughole. I want to go with the water. I want to be the water. Gone. Nothing. But I can't. I'm here in this bath. My sadness and fears are eating away at me and I'm getting bored of being in this state of nothingness. I get out of the bath, get dressed. I'm hungry and I'm ready for some fun. I want to eat and I want to play. I'm not sure what I want to do first but I know I want to forget about the badness and get on with the goodness, so I'm all up for games.

'Hey, Kim, you want to play a game?'

'No, I've got homework to do.'

'Can't I help you?'

'Yah, right. Go play some snooker with Dad.'

A big slap of silence.

'I've already done that.'

'Well I can't help.'

'Thanks for nothing.'

I go outside, kick a ball for a while, get bored, play with my dolls in their doll's house, see what Anna is cooking for dinner and eventually settle down to watch TV. *Maya the Bee* is on, and I happily slip into Maya's world of pollen, flowers and song.

I've started acting and doing plays. The best thing about acting is I get to be other things: animals, trees, I even get to play a cat. I am not scared of being in front of people, I love it, and I love the attention. I just do my thing, purr and wave my make-believe tail. I remember all my lines and never want it to end. I want to be that cat forever. After the show everyone comes up to me and tells me how good I am. Dad puts me high on his shoulders, he is so proud of me; he carries me all over and tells everyone I am his daughter. I am so happy. I believe he will never hurt me again, never touch me in dark places; this one night I am his daughter, he is my father and I love him. My mom, perfect mom, walks behind us smiling. We are the best family in the whole world. No one can ever be as happy as us. I am the cat that got the cream, lucky me, lucky nine-year-old me.

School is so hard. I can't concentrate for long; everything they teach me is too boring. I'm bad at maths, I can't spell anymore, and teachers find me a disruption in class. When I'm at home Dad doesn't let me leave my room until I learn my times tables. Mom agrees; she doesn't want a stupid daughter. So I'm stuck in my room looking at the numbers moving around the page. They make me dizzy as I force them into my head. I want to keep them there long enough so that I can recite them to Dad before I vomit them out of my brain.

I want to kiss my boyfriends and girlfriends when they come over to play and I'm touching myself a lot. It's so nice, so horrible; I feel bad and good at the same time. I like the feeling and can make myself twinkle at the end, but it only lasts a few seconds. Afterwards I lie there feeling nothing, numb, except for my beating heart accompanied by the sound of the old ladies cackling at me.

I'm nine, I'm a liar, I'm an actress and I'm Dad's favourite girl. I've started doing a lot of children's theatre productions. It began when my class went to watch *Jack and the Beanstalk*. I knew I didn't want to be watching, I wanted to be performing and so my passion truly began. After the play my mom spoke to the director of the company, she asked me to audition and I made the grade.

My first play is *Winnie the Pooh*, and I am Roo. I love it so much and make so many friends. I especially love the adult actors in the production. My favourite is an actor named Michael, and we also perform in *Noddy*, *The Wizard of Oz* and *Oliver!* together. Michael is so wonderful and caring, he makes me feel really special. I sit on his lap and chat for hours.

I like this world, acting and making an adult friend who isn't taking from me or hurting me. The strange thing I've learned about most adults is that they want to spoil all your fun, make something out of nothing and leave you feeling dirty, bad and guilty. Michael is different, he makes me feel so safe.

Then my mom gets a phone call from the director of the theatre company, telling her that I am sitting on Michael's lap and that I am being too loving towards him. This information is passed on to Dad and he confronts me. He is furious.

'What are you doing? Don't you know what strangers can do to you? You could get hurt. You mustn't sit on Michael's lap, he is not your father.'

'I'm sorry.'

'Sorry is not enough.'

As punishment, Dad doesn't speak to me. I go back to the theatre company and don't talk to Michael. I'm scared of him now and think he is like Dad. I feel bad, dirty and guilty, and I need to sort out the bad with Dad.

My options are:

1. *Talk to him, tell him I'm sorry and that I won't sit on anyone's lap again.*
2. *Stand naked and cold in front of Dad and make him happy.*

Number two seems to be my only option. It is the only way he will forgive me. A week has gone by without Dad speaking to me and I can't take it anymore; I have to take control of the situation.

Touching happens every day now, sometimes in the mornings, sometimes at night, on weekends and during the day. Dad's touching-me moments don't take up much time, maybe fifteen minutes in his busy twenty-four-hour day. When Dad's not touching me I am touching myself.

I am also praying a lot to G-d. I'm not sure if he is Jewish or Christian, I just know that he is out there listening to everyone's stories. He must have an amazing ability to remember everyone and love us all. When Mom was married to Lionel we were Jewish, I even went to a Jewish nursery school and celebrated Pesach and Rosh Hashanah. We ate matzah and gefilte fish. Then Mom married Dad and we became Christian, or should I say Christmas people, as Gran is the only one who goes to church. We don't talk about religion in my family and I don't mind, as long as I know G-d is my friend. Sometimes I think he must be too busy with other things to take care of me, but I carry on praying just in case one day he listens.

Mom and Dad have bought a house at the Vaal River. It reminds me of a tree house: it's beautiful, small and has a thatch roof. To get to my room I have to climb up a rope ladder. I love our little house and I love being at the river. We have a boat and I'm learning to water-ski. It's the biggest boat on the river and Dad called it Agape, which he tells me means G-d's love for humanity. It took me a couple of tries to stand up on two skis, but now I've got the hang of it and Dad is so proud of me. I love it when he is proud of me, I feel on top of the world. Impressing Dad feels like I'm impressing G-d, and that feels good.

Dad can be mean to Mom but she doesn't say anything. Sometimes he forces her to drive the boat while she cries. She hates arguing with him. She is always trying to keep the peace and make him feel like her king. Mom and I are Dad's subjects. Kim's not really involved in the family. Most weekends, she sleeps out at her girlfriends'. Dad doesn't mind. They're not soul connected. Kim sees him as her stepdad. I see him as a step above the rest.

The days at the Vaal are long and lazy. We eat, ski, sleep, my mom cooks, Dad drives the boat and the tractor. When dad is on a mission to touch me, he takes me to the garages behind the boat club. Dad holds my hand tight and I follow my pied piper into the large, dark, musty room. Dad disappears and his dark friend enters. I also leave, looking for a speck of light. Like a moth I'll go to it and stay there until Dad's friend is done.

Afterwards we walk back to my mom. Our little house is glowing in the late afternoon sun. Mom has started making the salads for tonight's dinner.

'Hungry?' Mom asks, smiling.

'Very.'

Dad can never take away my appetite.

The best thing about going to the Vaal is that Romy has started coming over on the weekends. I love having her with us; she still holds my hand and tells me stories, and it's as if she never left. There are moments I feel very jealous of her because Dad has been paying her a lot of attention and is ignoring me. This makes me so mad, I'm not Daddy's little girl when Romy is around. She is more of a tomboy than me and is better at water-skiing. Dad likes this. I feel very lonely and lost and have decided to make a stand and never water-ski again. This backfires because Dad tells me if I don't water-ski then I'm not allowed on the boat. I have no idea why, but all of a sudden I am terrified of skiing and I am beginning to think that my body has become the boss of me. It can create a fear through me. I get into a big panic and can't explain it to anyone. It doesn't matter, though, because I'm not allowed on the boat anyway.

'Candy, come on, don't be like this, come water-skiing.'

Romy's being kind, I can't stand it. She's all tanned, blonde and has the bounciest curls and greenest eyes I've ever seen.

'No, I'm not skiing and it doesn't matter anyway because Dad won't let me on the boat.'

'You're being silly.'

I'm screaming in my head: I'm not being silly, I'm scared, I can't move. Can't you see? Are you blind? I respond with 'Whatever,' and walk off.

I make a friend. We go exploring and find a broken-down old caravan in one of the nearby caravan parks. The door is locked but we climb in through a window that is slightly open. We find a bed and sit down.

'Let's play a game,' I say.

'Okay.'

'I'm the daddy, you're the mommy.'

'Okay.'

I come close and put my mouth to hers, it feels small and cold. She responds and we kiss and touch. I like the feeling as we rub against each other. This feels good, nothing else exists, no mommy, no daddy and no Romy They've all gone off on the boat and will never come back. I don't care; I don't want them to come back. I kiss harder, touch harder, rub harder and make myself twinkle again. We're finished, lying there together, silent. I feel sick. I think the Devil entered my body and I'm bad, really bad. I get up off the bed.

'See you around,' I say, hoping never to see her again and climb out the window, praying that G-d wasn't watching.

I run and run and run until I can't run anymore. I'm bad and I hate my insides. I walk home slowly. When I get there they're all there laughing and chatting. I see we're going to have a braai.

'Have you stopped sulking?' Dad asks.

Romy's looking over at me, smiling, loving me. I hate her.

'If you've stopped sulking, come and join us.'

I have stopped sulking. I touched, ran and walked the sulk away.

I sit down and join in the laughter. I like my happy family. It's a warm evening and the river is still. I feel still. No more running tonight. I'm just going to sit and enjoy. Enjoy my happy family. I'm nine. I know the difference between good and bad and I am both.

still nine

My favourite colours are blue, green and white. Is white a colour? I like blue and green because they bring out my eyes. I like white because it makes me feel innocent.

I am nine and still the smallest in my class. My hair is dark brown and scruffy. I like to swim even though I'm not very good at it and I'm still a mascot for school sports events (it's better that way because my short legs mean I'm not very fast). Mom comes to all my events. She always looks perfect, hair never out of place, outfits showing off her best assets. Mom looks good in bright colours, especially pinks and bright sun yellows. I also like her in blue because her eyes are just like mine and blue makes them look shiny and happy.

'You look so much like your mom.'

'Thanks,' I say, grinning.

My mom laughs louder than all the other moms, she also talks the most, she makes everyone feel good. I watch my mom talking to all the other mothers: she is so beautiful and I wonder if I'll look like her when I grow up. I wonder if Daddy loves me the way he does because I look like Mommy, and I wonder if looking like Mommy is a good thing, after all.

Things I've learned at nine:

1. *Adults lie.*
2. *My mom laughs the loudest but is sometimes the most unhappy.*
3. *Beauty is dangerous.*
4. *Learning lines for plays is easy.*
5. *School sucks.*
6. *The best way to keep secrets is to pretend you know nothing.*
7. *I don't like tomatoes.*
8. *I love movies.*
9. *I want my hair to grow.*
10. *I'm damn pretty, pretty sad.*

I'm moving schools because I've been struggling badly. I can't spell or do maths, my oral reading has gone downhill, I'm disruptive in class, play too rough and can't concentrate. So it's off to an educational psychologist for me.

'Are you happy?'

'Yes,' I say.

'Do you love your stepdad?'

'Yes.'

'Can you draw your family for me?'

I draw Mommy, Gran, Romy, Kim and myself very small and Dad as big as a bear.

'Wow, you must really love your stepdad!'

'Yes.'

Session over.

I'm a slow learner and must go to remedial school. I am prescribed Ritalin for my overactive behaviour and enrolled at Bellavista (a school for the not so fast – and I don't mean running). The Ritalin makes me crazy. I'm too chatty, have too much energy and am way too boisterous. I am taken off the Ritalin, and my new school life begins.

I actually like Bellavista: it is smaller with fewer kids in the class and the teachers are kind. Well, most of them. Especially Mr Baxter, whom I love. He has a round moon face and a bald head except for the sides, and laughs at all my jokes. I could hug him all day, which I do a lot of, just not all the time. He's the round version of the dad I've never had.

Teachers are beginning to notice that I'm hanging on to Mr Baxter. They don't like it; they don't like it at all. A quick phone call sorts it all out. Headmaster speaks to Mom, Mom speaks to Dad and Dad speaks to me.

'Candice, what are you doing?'

'What do you mean?'

'Why are you always hugging Mr Baxter?'

'He's my teacher and he's nice.'

'Well, stop it. Just stop it. Don't you know what men can do? You could get hurt. He's not your boy-friend.'

'Okay. I'm sorry.'

'Sorry is not good enough. Just stop it and do your school work.'

'Okay.'

I hate Mr Baxter and he is now my enemy. He is bad and I am scared of him. Tomorrow I won't talk to him, look at him or answer questions in class. I'll just be my school book, the ink, the paper, the tree before it was the paper.

Bad Mr Baxter, bad Candice.

Thank goodness for weekends: they are my favourite, especially in the summer. We always drive to the river on a Friday evening and spend the whole weekend in our swimming costumes. We run, we sleep, we eat and we play. I am still banned from the boat but I don't really care anymore, as I don't like water-skiing. I go on long walks by myself and imagine I'm going to marry Michael J. Fox. I also talk to the flowers and hug the trees.

List of the good and the bad at the Vaal River:

Good

1. *Breakfast of fried eggs and bacon.*
2. *Long days.*
3. *Games.*
4. *Playing in our caravan at the back of our house.*
5. *The cafe nearby that sells the best salt and vinegar crisps and toffees.*
6. *Holding Romy's hand and going for long walks while she tells me stories.*

Bad

1.   *Dad touching me there.*
2.   *Dad forcing me to lick his hard-on.*
3.   *Dad making me kiss him with my tongue.*
4.   *Dad licking me down there.*

School is going well. I'm captain of the netball team in which I play centre, I've made some good friends, I'm doing better than I was when I was at Linksfield, all the teachers like me, I'm not scared of Mr Baxter anymore, and I get an A for effort on my school report.

I like being nine. Soon I'll be old enough to leave home and start a new life. Maybe I'll change my name, go to a place where no one has been hurt, where people are good and animals are your best friends.

'Stop it. Please don't hit me.'

SMACK.

'Dad, I'm sorry.'

'Not sorry enough.'

'Please stop, it wasn't me.'

'Stop lying.'

SMACK. SMACK.

I stop crying. I am too sore and I don't care anymore. Silence.

SMACK. SMACK. SMACK.

I start talking to myself, 'Go on, hit me. Can't you see I'm strong, stronger than you?'

I think my silence stops Dad and he walks out of my bedroom. I am left alone, my loud pumping heartbeat and my angry head have joined my body in hate. The three of us will survive, we'll beat this man I call Dad.

It all started because one of my schoolteachers phoned my mom and told her I'd written in a textbook. Mom told Dad, Dad confronted me. I said I didn't do it and this made him furious. The rest is history.

A few days later the teacher phoned Mom and told her it wasn't me. Mom told Dad, Dad didn't bother to apologise, and the incident was over, never to be spoken of again. Dad's moods are starting to bore me, and instead of feeling afraid I'm starting to get mad.

I love the pretending of acting. If you play a fairy, you become one; if you act like a rag doll, you are one. It's the best escape ever.

A fairy plus a gnome plus a rag doll plus a Roo does not equal Candice Derman.

I love playing Pac-Man; maybe one day I'll be a champion.

I also love long summer days and afternoon thunderstorms. The thunderstorms wash away the heat of the day and bring coolness to the night. I like it when the night is cool; the cool eases my warm sweaty body, it eases my panic. Lately I've been waking up at two in the morning and falling asleep at about four. These hours are paralysing and I feel such fear. The house is silent, everyone is asleep and I keep having thoughts that someone will break in and attack my family. In these frightful two hours I can't move, I hear loud noises, laughter and silent echoes and then eventually I manage to fall asleep again. I wake up at six, get ready for school and am raring to go.

A new day, no one attacked us. Silly me, silly, silly me.

Some days I wonder if I've made it all up, wonder if Dad has never touched me and if it's all been a nightmare. I get so confused on a love day when Dad tells me I'm beautiful, I'm clever and he's so proud I'm his daughter. I love it when he tells me that even though he's not my biological parent, he loves me like a father would love his daughter. On these days I melt into the love and feel all dreamy, cloud blue and pink.

It's easy to keep a bad secret; I'm not bursting to tell anyone. I'd rather pretend to be a part of Mom's white-picket-fence fantasy. I'm so good at pretending, even I believe in happily ever after.

I sit on Dad's lap, pleased as Punch, a princess with an invisible tiara. My stepbrother, Richard, asks me if I know about the birds and the bees. I don't answer and get a confused look on my face.

Dad to the rescue, 'Come on, Candice doesn't know about that stuff.'

I look at Dad. He winks, a private wink between the two of us.

I play along. 'The birds and the bees, what do you mean?'

They laugh and run off, leaving me on the lap of my strong, loving dad.

I feel his private getting hard. 'Soon I'll show you about the birds and the bees,' Dad says, kissing my forehead. My invisible tiara clatters to the floor.

I smile, terror behind the grin.

Things I love at nine:

1. *Touching myself.*
2. *Gum.*
3. *Acting.*
4. *Ice cream.*
5. *Spare ribs.*
6. *Netball.*
7. *Kissing girls.*
8. *Movies.*

Things I hate at nine:

1. *Touching myself.*
2. *Secrets.*
3. *Night-time.*
4. *Fighting.*
5. *Vegetables.*

I open my legs and look down at my flower. I believe she is evil: she feels things I don't want to feel, and she makes me touch myself and demands the twinkle. How can a place where you wee from cause so many problems; why does Dad like her so much; why does she have different moods?

I look in the mirror, into my eyes. I think they are pretty but when I start looking longer, I think they are sad, ugly and hold a secret they can't reveal. I close my eyes, get up and walk away from the mirror. I don't want to see the saddest girl in the world. I promise not to look at myself again for too long. I'm such a good actress; even when I'm not in a play, I'm acting. No one knows my dark secret; they all think I'm the happiest girl in the world and that's the way it must stay.

I have a new problem: I've started to worry if people are cross with me. It's a terrible feeling and most of the time I spend wondering if I've said or done something wrong. I've started to go around asking all my friends and teachers if they are cross with me.

'Sarah, are you cross with me?'

'Why are you always asking everyone that, Candice?'

'I'm sorry, I can't help it.'

'That's stupid and the more you ask, the more annoying you become.'

I don't get it. Why can't people be gentle and kind and just answer, 'Of course not Candice, you're the sweetest girl in the world.' I'd say that to someone who kept asking, even if she wasn't the sweetest girl in the world. I guess I'm a master liar. I try not to ask anymore but I have to know. I walk in fear and hate it and no one can help me.

So my days are kept busy with wondering who's cross with me, doing my homework, acting in plays and having fun. My nights are filled with fear and darkness, Dad's 'cuddles' and sleep that doesn't come easily. Who said being a child was easy?

ten

The big one zero. Hello world it's me, Candice Derman. I'm a tiny bit taller, my hair is a little longer, and my eyes, well, I'm not sure. I try not to look into them but they do seem bluer. Everyone tells me I'm blooming, and I'm becoming aware of how good looks can get you further in life. This is not going unnoticed by Dad and he is starting to enjoy the new me.

'Candice, you really are going to be the most beautiful woman in the world.'

'Thanks, Dad.'

The strange thing about being pretty is that it doesn't really make me feel better. It's not the same for Mom, who seems to enjoy her beauty, the compliments from women and looks from men. My mom dolls herself up with make-up, hair colour and beautiful clothes. Maybe one day I'll understand this, but right now all my prettiness seems to do is make Dad want to hurt me.

My relationship with Dad has gone from strength to strength.

We have a few games we like to play:

INDESCRIBABLE

1. *Grabbing my hair and banging my head on the table. I let him do it. I have no choice. It's a bit of fun; Dad plays rough and I fight back. It's damn sore but I laugh loudly and make him bang my head again and again and again. I get headaches, but I don't show any pain in my face, I just smile. Over time the banging gets harder and my inner self now has a new dialogue: 'You won't get me,' I say, over and over again as my head hits the table. I laugh again. No one is winning; better that than if Dad won.*

2. *Love bites. Dad starts by blowing raspberries on my neck and bottom in front of everyone. Over time the blowing becomes a private game of sucking and he sucks and sucks. I just laugh because tears won't make him stop anyway.*

3. *Drowning me in the pool. This is the worst game and I try not to let him do it. I am so scared of going under the water. Dad dunks me, holds me under and just as I start to gag he brings my head out of the water. I breathe quickly, desperately, forcing a fixed grin before he pushes me down again. 'Please not again,' I gasp, 'not again.' These games become part of our daily ritual.*

I'm learning new tricks to get through the darkness:

1. *Hold your breath till you can't anymore.*
2. *Pretend you're dead.*
3. *Count very fast.*

4. *Keep telling yourself you're stronger than this.*
5. *Believe you are a princess and one day your prince will come.*

It's not strange for a daughter to be alone with her dad, to go with him to his office, sit on his lap or go to the movies together. Nor is it strange for a dad to kiss his daughter goodnight, play in the pool with her or to take her for walks alone.

What is strange is what Dad does to me during what he calls our special time.

It's an odd feeling to come from a big family and yet to feel so alone. I'm like a superhero with a mask, my real life unknown. No one sees the hiding; they see the clown, the joker and the comedian. I only have myself to blame; I hide my identity and my secrets so well, behind my heart, at the back of my brain and down in my spirit, which has become a dark hole.

Is there a place where children don't get hurt? My perfect ten-year-old life is being overshadowed by the danger of Dad. He has my whole family under his spell as they walk like zombies doing everything he says. My mom doesn't see the signs; she doesn't know what lurks behind her back. Mommy, my beautiful mommy, with her eyes tightly closed, has she fallen asleep?

I have Dad's penis in my mouth, so hard I want to choke. I hate him; maybe I could bite it off. I close my eyes, use one of my tricks to leave the room, leave this place, and leave Dad's hardness in my mouth. I count and count and I hold my breath, pretend I'm dead. I get pins and needles and have to breathe.

I dream of my prince, I see him; I imagine him and I feel better. My invisible tiara is back on my head.

One day my prince will come, and until then I will:

1. *Dream.*
2. *Wish.*
3. *Pray.*
4. *Play.*
5. *Love.*
6. *Hope.*
7. *Act.*

I'm not trying to be happy or sad, feelings well up in me. I'm many emotions all squashed into one. I'm not just a girl who is broken; I'm a girl with a secret, but the secret is not me.

I'm ten. The Devil sits at the end of my bed, but that doesn't mean G-d's not sitting with me too.

Dad comes. He feels better.

'Dinner,' Mom calls from upstairs.

'Coming …'

It's Sunday night, and Mom and Dad are having friends over. Mom has prepared an amazing spread: meats, cheeses, breads and dips. It's delicious. I'm starving.

Romy, Kim, Mommy, Daddy, Gran and I sit like a happy family, joking and laughing. Their friends think we are the luckiest family in the world. We have each other, love, money, beauty, a house at the river, a luminous green Porsche Carrera, a Mercedes and a Jeep. We live in a mansion with tennis courts and wear beautiful clothes. We've got to be the luckiest family alive and I believe them: I am lucky, I have everything I could ask for.

Next year I'll be eleven and maybe that will be an even luckier year and Dad will stop the licking, the fingering and the touching. Maybe we will become a real father and daughter. That's what I wish for, more than all the flowers in the world, more than all the stars in the sky and more than all the people on earth. I love Dad so much. I bite into my meat and cheese sandwich. I love this sandwich, all the different tastes and textures, the softness, the sweetness, the saltiness; I never want to stop eating it.

I also hate Dad so much, more than all the flowers in the world, more than all the stars in the sky and more than all the people on earth. I look over at Dad, all talk and smiles, and I realise I'm so confused. I look at him long and hard; he doesn't notice. It's like I freeze him, I see his dark hair, each one in its place, his olive skin, his dark brown eyes, one with a freckle in the white of it, I see his nose hair, his ear hairs, I look at him and I decide I love him. He doesn't mean to hurt me, and one day he'll stop. I finish my sandwich and join in the jolliness. After all, a girl's got to do what a girl's got to do. Life in my kingdom can be fun.

Tuesday night is Dad's tennis night with his friends. Dad's tanned skin shines against the white he wears from head to toe. The world is attracted to Dad; he is smart, good-looking and charming. Dad makes a man feel like a man, and a woman glow in his light. Dogs love him, cats love him, my mom and sisters love him and I love him. Tennis night gives Dad's girls a chance to giggle. He is with his friends, working up a sweat, and Mom has a joy in her stiletto step as she prepares another spread that makes my tummy roar: bagels, cream cheese and caviar. Caviar is one of my favourite things.

How could I hurt this perfect family?

If I spoke the words, 'Mom, Dad is touching me,' her world would come tumbling down, Mom's fantasy would become a lie and I would lose her down the rabbit hole. Dad would go to jail, my sisters would be broken and it would all be my fault.

If I spoke the words, 'Mom, Dad is touching me,' I would lose control. I can cope with the lie but I'd go mad with the truth. I need to hide the darkness. I must put the evil away, it's tennis night, my mom is the star, some of her girls are with her and we are one big, happy family.

eleven

He enters me, sitting on the tiles in the shower, me over him, my short legs on either side of his body. The pain is excruciating, his large, hard, long snake in my small tight hole.

I am naked. I have no pubic hair and have not started growing breasts. His hands cup either side of my bottom and he pulls me up and down. The water is going in my mouth and eyes. We are on holiday in Port Alfred. Most of my family is here, running around somewhere in this huge holiday home. I can't do any of my tricks: float away from myself, become an object or hold my breath. I am trying, trying hard but the pain is too sharp and I can't run away from it. Dad is moaning silently, no one can hear, he looks in ecstasy. My face does not mirror his, I'm trying to make it expressionless. It's difficult to do.

I wonder if I'm bleeding, but I won't look down; later I'll know. It happens quickly; cruelty only needs a few minutes. He moves me up and down faster and faster and then his goo explodes inside me. He groans, his body goes limp for a few seconds and I just sit there on top of him, waiting, wondering what's next, his hands still cupping my bum. He lifts me off him and his penis leaves my hole. Is my body still intact?

He effortlessly puts me to one side of him. I feel as light as a feather, as see-through as plastic, my body feels as thin as paper.

Abuse is cold, hard, out of control. It's the wrong side of masculine and there is no sign of feminine. It's muscle, it's fat, it's hairy, hard and sweaty, then cold all over again. It's animal, there's no kindness and no end; it's the Devil or the Devil's friend. Abuse takes without caring, there are no consequences and no rules. Abuse turns a man into an evil king, a crocodile, a vagina cannibal. Abuse has no taste buds, no colour, no sound. Abuse is a silent living hell.

'Wasn't that wonderful?' Dad mumbles.

I'm speechless, I'm eleven, and this is the beginning of the rest of my life, this horrible, dark small life.

Close your eyes, Candice, close them, I tell myself. Breathe, Candice, breathe, I tell myself. Pray, Candice, pray, I tell myself. To whom, I ask, as it doesn't seem like G-d's around; it doesn't matter, I answer. I pray and it helps.

Dad picks me up, hugs me and we step out of the shower. I'm drying myself. Any blood? I won't look down, not yet, not ever.

Holidays are the best: the beach, the sea, the sun, the sand, the happy holidaymakers, everyone is happy on holiday. All the happiness is neatly parcelled up during the year, ready for the holidays, and then unwrapped when Mom is tanning or when Romy and I are jumping in the waves, holding hands and laughing. Romy and I are as brown as berries and wear matching costumes. We love pretending we're twins, even though she is older, taller and skinnier than me. We feel so complete when we're together, I don't feel jealous or hurt when Dad isn't around. I feel like the two of us make up our very own family.

I don't kiss girls anymore, that urge has gone; but I still touch myself, that urge hasn't gone. I start to notice boys. I know I'm young but everything started early for me. I now know first-hand about the birds and the bees and I'm hoping to meet a bee that loves me. I'm eleven and I'm on the lookout.

My new wishes:

1. *To meet a boy. We run away and move to a caravan by the sea.*
2. *Romy and I run away and live in a caravan by the sea.*

Romy will never know my secret and I don't mind; I don't want her to be upset or to feel bad. Anyway, all the laughing and playing helps me to forget, and loving my sister the way I do makes all the bad go away and life seem as lovely and as heart-warming as a cupcake.

Mommy is still the most beautiful woman I have ever seen and the older I get, the more people tell me I'm exactly like her. I am becoming happier about this because the more I look like her, the sooner I'll catch my man and leave.

Eleven is like being twenty, only you're eleven.

Things an eleven-year-old should be able to do:

1. *Leave school.*
2. *Get a job.*
3. *Have a boyfriend.*
4. *Talk back.*
5. *Be able to live alone.*
6. *Eat whenever they want to.*

I think if a girl is being forced to have sex, there shouldn't be rules. Dad makes me go to bed at nine o'clock, do my homework, doesn't let me watch age-restricted movies. I'm not even allowed to have boyfriends or to sleep out. I'm silently starting to rage.

I go to a lot of extra classes. You could call me a specialist in extra lessons.

1. *Extra Afrikaans.*
2. *Extra maths.*
3. *Extra spelling.*
4. *Extra drama.*

Of course, I love the drama classes, but the rest suck. I'm not sure why I have to learn Afrikaans and who really cares about maths and so what if I can't spell.

ELEVEN

The more extra classes I do, the more I switch off and start to daydream.

My favourite daydreams are:

1. *I'm a famous actress and I can do what I want and say what I feel.*
2. *I'm stuck in a sweet shop and eat all the sweets I possibly can. The colours of the sweets and the colours of the shop make me dizzy with happiness.*
3. *Everyone in the world loves me, thinks I'm special, clever, beautiful and talented. That's the world I'd like to live in, the 'everyone thinks Candice is wonderful' world.*

My fanny is getting used to Dad's penis. It's not so sore anymore when he puts it inside me. The first few times the pain was extreme, like putting small tyres on a four-by-four, uncomfortable and wrong, but I'm learning that after a while everything can fit in life, even if it's a push or a shove. You can get it to do what you want it to do.

My whole eleven-year-old self feels like a push and a shove. I make friends but I feel like I'm pushing them to like me; I try to learn maths but I feel like I'm shoving the information into my brain. Nothing comes easily to me.

Dad shoves his tongue in my mouth and pushes his penis inside my hole, more shoving and pushing. I'm lying naked in my mom's bed, my pyjama pants crumpled around my ankles. The sunflowers on them were bright yellow once, large and proud, but not anymore; now they are squashed and faded and I can only just make out the yellow.

'Candice, don't feel bad, you know G-d understands my love for you. It's so deep and I can't help myself, you understand me.'

What is he talking about? I hear nothing, I understand nothing, I look down at my pyjama pants and see the faded yellow. All I want to do is hide inside the sunflower and fade away with it.

'What about Mommy?'

'She wouldn't understand; you can never tell anyone. You would destroy this family, I'd go to jail, and do you want me to go to jail?'

Silence. 'No.'

'Good.'

I imagine my face, my expression, my blue eyes. Are they watering? Are they cold? Why does Dad not see I'm broken?

After he's come I leave the bed, pull up my sunflower pyjama pants, put on my top and leave the bedroom. I bathe myself, although I can't wash away the internal dirt, and get ready for my day.

Dad's got a movie planned. I can't help myself, I'm excited: movies are my favourite and I love the smell of popcorn and icy raspberry drinks.

'My treat, just the two of us.'

I know his act of unkindness has been done so we will have a great day. I'll eat all the popcorn I possibly can, and drink all my raspberry ice drink until my tummy freezes and I get that icky-comfy-full-yummy-yuck feeling.

We watch *Back to the Future* with Michael J. Fox. He is so cute, the movie is great, and I end up having a wonderful day with Dad. He gives me lots of good attention; the kind dads should give their daughters. Everyone tells Dad how lovely I am and I see him glowing. That makes me glow, knowing how proud he is of me.

'Not only is she pretty, but she's so talented. One day she'll be a well-known actress.'

I blush. I love Dad, I love belonging to someone, and I love being loved so much. Dad is definitely two people: the best father in the world and the worst father in the world. My mind is learning to separate the two; to love the good moments and to breathe through the bad, or simply stop breathing. I find either way works.

Dad and I go home, full and happy. Mommy, perfect Mommy, is waiting for us.

'Dinner is ready. Chutney chicken and rice.'

Romy lives with us now and she is waiting at the dining-room table with Kim and Gran.

I think to myself that I must be the craziest eleven-year-old in the world, because I get so down and mad and yet here I am sitting for dinner in my big house with my pretty, perfect family. All of us laughing, happy, innocent and naïve, while deep down far,

far away, locked inside me I know I hate them all. I must be made of something bad because they are all so lovely. I lock the feeling away, breathe in my love for the only family I've got, the only family I want, the only family I know. I breathe out the bad me and watch my badness sail away past my family, over Dad's head, out the door, and I hope never to see that me again.

That me, the bad me, does go for a few weeks and I feel at ease, happy and carefree. Dad's been away on business so there's no nonsense down there. I can't help wondering if dogs do it with puppies, sheep with lambs, cats with kittens or lions with cubs. These are questions I start asking myself, but as soon as I do, I feel an uncomfortable dread and push myself to think of other things.

Other questions I ask myself:

1. *Is blue still my favourite colour?*
2. *Am I going to buy a hotdog at break?*
3. *Does Sarah still think I'm her best friend?*

These questions are less bothersome, and slowly the unease leaves my body. I also have answers for all these questions.

I'm training my mind to go from bad thoughts to good thoughts. Sometimes it works and sometimes it doesn't. Today it did. My 'life is cherry' mood is back. The nice thing about life is that sometimes you do have the answers when you're stuck, and you can move forward and just sip on a frozen raspberry drink.

Mom's delighted when Dad comes back from his business trip. She loves feeding him and making him happy and full. She gets up early to make him breakfast: eggs, bacon, a fresh pot of coffee and a whole lot of love. I see Mom wanting to please Dad, the twinkle in her eye when he sits at the table and her excitement when he makes appreciative noises about her food. Mom has no idea Dad is a wolf in disguise; she is just so happy, she thinks she has won a prize. Mom loves Dad, Dad loves Mom and they both love me.

Eleven is terribly confusing. I'm almost a teenager, I run around like a hooligan but I like to wear dresses. I feel afraid of the dark and would love my mom to cradle me in her arms, but I'd also like to have a boyfriend and leave home. I've just got to sit still, hold these feelings inside and decide whether to breathe or not.

Things I love at eleven:

1. *Caviar.*
2. *Training bras.*
3. *Ice-skating.*
4. *Sunshine.*
5. *Fruit.*
6. *Sleepovers.*
7. *Netball.*
8. *Michael J. Fox.*
9. *Dad.*

INDESCRIBABLE

Things I hate at eleven:

10. Loneliness.
11. Cheese blintzes.
12. Maths.
13. Fighting.
14. Confusion.
15. Sex.
16. Dad.

Eleven is hard and eleven is easy.

twelve
going on thirteen

I'm in my dad's office; he is doing me on the floor. My bony back is jutting into the rough carpet, I'm naked on top, bra cast away to the side, skirt crumpled around my waist, and panties pulled down to my knees. Dad's trousers are around his knees, his shirt wrinkled and sticking to his sweaty, musty body. He is thrusting in and out and I'm wondering if he remembered to lock the door. Part of me wishes someone would walk in and see this unholy sight; and part of me is in fear that someone would see me, legs open, my eyes wide and terrified, with a full view of Dad's ass and balls.

That someone could be Jodi, who has started working with Dad and has also moved back home. If she opened the door maybe I would be saved, she could be G-d's chosen one. But Dad doesn't make mistakes: he would never leave the door unlocked, he would never let us get caught.

When Dad is on top of me my body responds, wet, hot, cold, stone. My head shouts, 'Go away, motherfucker', but no voice comes out. I'm naked, weak and pathetic, hating me, blaming me, shouting at me, 'You stupid girl, do something.' But I lie there, I just lie there, allowing my dad to be in charge. Abuse takes away my fight, my cheek, my love of me.

I look up at his desk and I see a photo of my mom smiling down, with her blue eyes and big, wide toothy grin. It is a pretty picture of her and I wonder what her expression would be if she could see her husband and daughter now. I watch the expression on my mom's face change: I see her blue eyes turn murky and her lips turn downward, she clenches her jaw and I wonder if her expression shows blame. I wonder if she would blame Dad or me. I blink, look away, look at the photo again; she is still smiling, happy and unaware.

Dad comes, gets up and gives me a hand, kind man. We clean up; tissues are always close at hand. He unlocks the door and carries on with business as usual. Of course I do the same; there is homework to be done and I want my dad to be proud of me. He sits at the head of the desk and I sit opposite him, just like a regular daughter and father.

My dad wears a watch, cufflinks, a tie around his thick neck for business meetings and a gold ring on his pinky finger, which he tells me is a family heirloom. He loves movies about historical figures, and *Ben Hur* and *Spartacus* are among his favourites. He watches nature documentaries, lions attacking zebras, a hyena eating a buck, or a snake swallowing a rabbit. My dad can shoot a gun and speak a couple of languages. He also tells me he can parachute out of a plane. He disciplines the misbehaved, has neat handwriting and quotes paragraphs from self-help books. He can unzip his trousers, pull his underpants to the side, take out his penis and come all in five to ten minutes. My dad is multi-talented and has many faces.

Twelve is a funny coming of age. For starters, I'm changing physically and if I stand naked in front of a full-length mirror, I see short dark hairs growing on my legs and my privates. My breasts are also growing; they're pert, round and pretty and I like them. I'm also scared of them. They seem so grown up and I'm not sure I want to be a grown-up.

My curly hair has started to grow and my curls have dropped and look like dancing springs around my face. The plumpness in my cheeks is less and I have visible cheekbones now.

I do a few looks in the mirror, conveying different moods. First happy – I grin, large, too large, exposing my top and bottom teeth. I look silly but this makes me smile. Next a grumpy face – I frown so much I push my brows right down into my eyes. Then a sad face – I make my mouth fall to the ground and my eyes well up with tears. I like the sad face, it helps me release something deep inside me and I crumble to the floor and cry.

I cry because I'm lost, I cry because I love life, I cry because I hate Dad, I cry because it feels good, I cry because my eyes tell me the truth and force me to stop lying when I'm alone in my silence. I cry because I can. Naked and alone, I cry.

Dad's been going to Mozambique a lot. We have a furniture business in Mozambique and two wood mills on the island of Pemba just off the coast. These trips give me time off from sex and I can become the real me, the naughty me, the cheeky me, the one who fears nothing and likes to play, because when the cat's away the mouse will play. I decide on some serious play, sleep over at friends, friends sleep over with me, talking until all hours of the morning, having midnight feasts, going to the movies, flirting with boys, putting on new bras for my new boobs, and taking my new high school by storm.

I've just turned thirteen and started at Wendywood High School, a school for the normal, not for the slow. This is a big jump for someone who's been in a remedial school and I'm excited and nervous about it. I know how to pretend well but I don't know how to pretend I'm good at school. It's so crap being abused and struggling at school, I feel like I can never win.

I sit in class and listen to the teachers in a complete blur. I feel like I'm slowly rafting down a river, watching the birds flying over me, seeing the trees rustling on the bank. It seems like a perfect day and I smile, but behind my frozen smile I know there is a massive drop coming. I know I'm going to fall and drown but my smile remains frozen. My teachers must find me so sweet but terribly dim.

The problem with struggling at school is that you can't fake it and I'm doing so badly the teachers are starting to notice. There are other kids struggling too, so they start a class for the ones who aren't managing. Not so great to be moved into that class because the whole school knows that Standard 6D is for dummies. I try to make jokes and be the naughtiest in class, just so I don't have to think. Think equals fear.

In the looks department I'm not really confident, but people seem to like what they see and I have to use this to my advantage, which makes me seem arrogant and conceited. Rather that than feeling insecure and needy.

There's one boy in particular who doesn't mind arrogant and conceited. His name is Dale and he's ten out of ten in the looks department. Dale is a couple of years older than me and is in standard eight.

'Hey Candice, it's my birthday today.'

'Well, what do you want me to do? Sing for you?'

'That would be nice,' Dale says grinning.

'Yah right. See you around.' I'm playing hard to get. I walk away with butterflies in my tummy.

Dale's working hard to get me. All of a sudden he goes to the same extra maths teacher as me, he hangs out near me at break and in assembly he is in the front row of the balcony, looking down at me. I can't help turning my head and looking up at him. Dale's breaking me down. I have to catch my breath when I see him. Wendywood High is looking a lot more rosy with a sexy six-foot-two boy wanting me.

6D is also a better class to be in; at least we learn at a pace I can keep up with. Hopefully, this will help me to pass. I'm scared of knowing that I have so many years to go at school: five years feels like a lifetime and when every subject is a struggle, a lifetime seems like eternity.

Life sometimes feels like a blur; things happen so slowly and sometimes they happen so fast. I wake up, think about Dale, get ready for school and eat breakfast. I go to school, hear the teachers talking to me, chat to my friends, flirt with Dale. Go home, take off my school uniform, eat lunch, daydream about Dale. Dad sneaks a moment with me, undoes his zip, leaves his shirt and trousers on, undoes my skirt, licks his hand, slides it onto my vagina, makes her wet and slips his hard penis into me. I'm thinking to myself, 'Dad, I've got to do my maths homework.' Dad comes, one, two, three, trousers up, shirt tucked into trousers, and he leaves.

I'm somehow getting used to the normal, not normal, the fast, slow thing about my life. And the blur.

Dale and I start hanging out together at break. We talk about rugby. He's the captain of the school team and plays a mean game. We talk about movies. Dale loves Yul Brynner and westerns. We talk about our families. His parents are divorced and he only has one sister. Today Dale seems talked out. He's not saying much and I'm worried he's cross with me. I'm fumbling through a meaningless monologue, trying to fill the silence.

Eventually I take a breath and Dale interrupts me. 'Candice, I've got something to ask you.'

'Okay.'

'Do you want to be my girlfriend?'

'Really?' It feels like Dale's just asked me to marry him.

'Yes, really.'

'Of course I'll be your girlfriend.' I jump up and hug him. I'm ecstatic. This boy is mine.

A few weeks go by and Dad's not liking Dale. He's jealous that I'm floating on Dale's cloud nine. I'm often not allowed to go to Dale's house but luckily he's allowed to come to mine. I love spending time with my boyfriend, who somehow understands me.

Dale doesn't know about Dad: he doesn't know that after our young, fresh, beautiful kisses, I get an old tongue and a penis shoved inside me. I couldn't tell Dale; not me the virgin, the one who has never been touched.

Dale must be the first to touch my breasts, to kiss my stomach, to stroke my skin. Kissing Dale feels so good, Prince Charming kissing his princess. I feel so clean with Dale, so untouched.

'Want to go out tonight?'

'I can't, Dad won't let me.'

'What is it with your stepdad?'

'I don't know.' I want to scream out and tell Dale what Dad makes me do. I want to tell Dale how it makes me feel. I want Dale to hold me.

'Let's not talk about my dad, please. Let's just kiss.'

We do; we kiss for so long that I get lost in Dale's smell, in Dale's touch, in Dale's kisses. I look into his eyes and know another world is possible, a world where love exists, where hope happens and dreams are real. I know real love comes with no violence, it's not about fear and silence, it's not about having power over another person. It's soft and kind and intense and passionate, it's about giving and taking, discussing, and kissing and kissing and kissing. I know from this moment, from deep inside me, that one day I will escape Dad, escape this reality and live a life I can be proud of. Dad can never take away my desire to love or be loved, he can't take it away because I know love can heal. Loving Dale so hard is my therapy.

I feel my heart beating, I feel so excited and I know I'll escape. I kiss Dale harder.

'Dale, I love you.'

'I love you too, Candice.'

Dear G-d, please, please let this last forever. I pray.

Our relationship develops into something really special. We enjoy each other's company so much; life seems better with a boyfriend like Dale. I know I'm young but I feel years older, and somehow Dale seems so much more mature than his teenage years. I'm enjoying this, these special moments. I like pretending I'm a virgin who has never been touched; being a naïve teenager who is experiencing first love. I know the only truth in that sentence is that I'm experiencing my first love, but who cares.

Dale and I write a lot of letters to each other. His always start with love and praise, '*Candice I love you, you are so clever, it doesn't matter that you struggle at school, one day you are going to be a great actress. I love your body, you are beautiful.*' Mine always end with fear and insecurity, '*Dale do you really love me, do I turn you on, do you really think I'm clever?*'

I always ask and he always answers. His letters put me on a love high. I'm not floating above myself, not running away from my body, not watching me from a distance. I am connected, I'm floating with my body, I'm being me, in love with a boy who loves me back.

School continues to be difficult and sex with Dad seems to be getting more intense, but with Dale around it seems more bearable. I'm not excited about the school holidays that are coming up and having to go away with my family for three weeks. Three weeks without Dale scares me. Three weeks with Dad scares me.

San Lameer is lovely; it's by the beach and we're staying in a big holiday house. I like being at the beach, watching the never-ending skyline and imagining I am out on the water, floating in nothingness, just being one with G-d. If there is a G-d, of course, because I wonder if G-d would let small girls get hurt and big men enjoy it; I wonder why G-d doesn't help lost puppies and broken children.

I like to tan and go a deep chocolate brown. It makes me happy, makes me feel healthy and strong, like I'm a little brown weapon. This is stupid, of course, because I'm nothing of the sort. I'm just a small, brown, abused smudge, which is also stupid because I'm not that either. I'm really a small, brown, strong girl who now knows love and the difference between good and bad. I'm a girl who knows what I like. I like that Dale doesn't grab me roughly when we kiss, that he doesn't force his strong body on me. I like it when he tickles me softly and holds me lovingly. I like that I'm in control. I don't want sex, not yet anyway, I don't want this innocence to go. I want to like myself for a little longer. Sex ruins things, makes men greedy for more.

Dad is moving fast, in and out of me, licking my nipples, his arms on either side of me; my legs are open and limp. He is moaning, I am still, my nipples are hard and sore, not excited. My arms are spread out, I am not moaning. I am wet down there but it's not from excitement.

My mom is upstairs making breakfast for the family. It seems like this moment will never end, the ongoing fucking, the ongoing moving in and out. Maybe I'll be in this position for the rest of my life, grow old, and end up a haggard old lady. Maybe Dad will die on me and we will decompose as one.

I still try to float above us when he is moving in and out of me, but this morning I watch everything he is doing, somehow I can't turn my head away. I stare at Dad and me, the weak and the strong, the lion and the deer, the dead girl and the live man. Dad comes inside me. I'm so used to the smell of his smoker's breath, his sweaty body and his cum.

I wonder why I went to lie next to him, why I still look for love from him, why I let him do this, why I don't run away and why I can't just scream. But I'm left with nothingness inside my soul, the death of me even though I'm still alive, cum inside me from my dad. I'm left desperate, alone and guilty. I hate my inability to get up and start hitting him. I hate myself and I hate my life.

I'm falling off the universe and I can't watch me anymore, so I make a list of all the things I love in life. I rush through it so I don't drown in Dad's bodily fluids.

I love:

1.   *Dale.*
2.   *The ocean.*
3.   *Watching the sunrise and sunset.*
4.   *Acting and movies.*

I start to feel better. Time to put on my clothes and run and run and run, and pretend I'm not going to come back to my life, the life of Candice Derman, the fake, the liar, the oppressed, the victim.

My feeling better doesn't last long, as worry has moulded itself to resemble me. It starts in my heart, a massive deep beat, one thump at a time. I worry that I'm pregnant, that Dad could be the father of my child. I panic, I can't breathe. I'm on the beach, I'm on the white sand. Breathe Candice, breathe, it just takes one breath at a time. I'll ask Mom later, I'll make up a story; it will be fine, I'll be fine.

The sun is shining, the day is bright and my thirteen-year-old self is filled with doom and gloom. Night arrives, dinner is eaten and I manage to participate in family banter. Mom comes to say goodnight and I begin my story lie. I learn that a girl has to have started her periods to be able to have a baby, so I'm pregnancy free and Mom is none the wiser.

'Goodnight,' she kisses me on my forehead.

Good night it is.

Our holiday continues as if we're the happiest family in the world. The sun warms me up from the inside out and gives me a tan my friends will be jealous of. I buy African beads and granadilla ice lollies. I smile at all the right times and play happy families; Dad has me well trained. I even sometimes believe the lie. But behind this picture-perfect snapshot I am disfigured and ugly.

I'm growing up very confused, with mixed emotions swimming inside my body. I carry them with me daily and think that if I got on a scale and weighed myself, I'd be heavier for them.

The list of emotions I feel often (all mixed together like Smarties in a box, only not as much fun):

1. *Guilt.*
2. *Insecurity.*
3. *Anger.*
4. *Neediness.*
5. *Vulnerability.*
6. *Confusion.*

I am thirteen. I need lots of attention and find myself becoming louder than I need to be and naughtier than I want. I'm scared to be invisible and scared to be seen. My schoolwork is so bad and I wonder how I'm ever going to leave school. It's awful to fail at every subject and carry on pretending you're fine with all of it, laugh your way out of it or just act like you don't care. If you struggle at school, the number one rule is to pretend school is beneath you and you have better things to do. Of course, being thirteen and having better things to do doesn't convince my teachers, so my tactics are not so good after all. But who cares, I'm thirteen and I've got people to meet and things to do.

still

thirteen

'Your our body is looking so sexy.'

'Thanks, Dad.'

'You're going to have great boobs, my bet is they're going to be a big and firm C, perhaps even a D.'

I hate my breasts. Dad kisses my nipples; he has put on weight and his bloated body is on top of me. A whale of a man, I hate him. My vagina widens and gets wet; she lets him in so easily now, how quickly she betrays me. Dad turns me over. He is looking at my ass, which is also growing. I hate that, I don't want a big ass. I hate my body, I hate my curves.

'What a peach.' He sucks my bum.

Dad's taking his time today, he's not going to come quickly. He's enjoying the back of his thirteen-year-old daughter's body. I'm facing the bed and I'm looking at the wrinkled white sheet, the same sheet my mom sleeps on. I see the mattress, the mattress made of sponge. I look deeper, I see bed mites, I wish they'd bite me, eat me alive.

Dad explodes.

I'm back, turned over, I'm screaming in my head, I'm silent, I face my devil.

Mom and Dad aren't seeing eye to eye at the moment. There is so much fighting and so much anger. Their fights are about money, business, their relationship and my attitude. Mommy's upset most of the time. Sometimes she tries to grab Dad's gun to kill herself, which is followed by Gran speaking in tongues, praying that the Lord Jesus will stop my mom from blowing her brains out.

Mom, of course, never commits suicide. Jesus obviously helps.

When Dad's away, things settle and I go to school and act normal. My normal, naughty, nice, attention-deficient, energetic, loud and cheeky self, which calls for daily reports. Teachers write about my behaviour so they can keep me in check and to ensure that I don't deteriorate into an evil teenager.

'Candice, what's going on with you?'

'Nothing Mom, I'm fine.'

'Well it doesn't seem like it. I know you are smart, so buckle down and work hard. It will make your life so much easier.'

'I'll try Mom.'

'That's all I'm asking. Make your dad and me proud.'

I try to change the subject. 'Can I please go to see Dale on Saturday?'

'Only if you do your homework and behave in class.'

'I promise.'

'Fine, I'll drop you off in the morning before my hairdresser appointment.'

'Thanks Mom, I won't let you down.'

I spend a lot of my time doing what I don't want to do. I eat vegetables when I really want dessert, do PE when I really want to watch a movie, and have sex with Dad when I really want to be cuddling Dale. The only time I feel I'm doing what I want is when I'm with Dale.

Dale fills my heart and life. His love helps me with my balancing act between sanity and insanity. His large hands cup my face and he tells me he loves me. I believe him, his olive green eyes let me know. They speak of kindness and I feel so safe with him. I almost forget that I'm the girl with the dark secret. He's experienced a lot in his teenage life and knows how to love. He's smoked dagga, had sex with girls older than him, and can drive a car.

Dale is so cool, it's almost a crime.

But when he's with me it's as if I'm all that matters to him. He looks at me, Candice Derman, and wants to know me. What can I tell him?

I'm thirteen going on thirty, abused, used and tired. Or should I tell him about the Candice Derman who's with him now? The thirteen-year-old girl whose heart is beating with love. Should I tell him that I love him and don't want to leave him, that I never want to go home, want to stay with him forever, run away together?

'Dale, can I tell you something?'

'Of course Candice, you can tell me anything.'

'When the time is right I want you to be my first.'

Dale kisses me, 'Yes, when the time is right.'

I take his hand and slip it under my shirt and onto my breast. My heart is beating so fast, I am excited, he touches me so softly, my nipples go hard, my body loves Dale's touch, I am in heaven, nothing is bad. We kiss, we are caressing, we don't need to go any further, this is enough for now. I feel his hard bit in his pants but I am not afraid of him. I love Dale and I am allowing him to touch me in this way.

'Dale, do you really love me?'

'Why are you always asking me, Candice, can't you see? You need to believe me.'

I do believe him deep down, but I want to hear him tell me again. I want to believe it not only in the deepest parts of me but in the places I can go to quickly. I want to believe him in my skin, at the nape of my neck, in the shallow bits of me, so when Dad takes what he shouldn't I feel Dale whispering, I love you.

Mom, sexy Mom, drops me off at school in her drop-dead-gorgeous Porsche. The other kids are drooling. They can't believe their eyes. My beautiful mom with her beautiful aqua eyes, aqua Porsche, tight ass and big boobs. I'm the envy of them all, they look and they want. Boys have wet dreams about my mom, girls want my mom as their best friend and everyone wants my life. How sad for them that I can't offer it to them. How sad for them that they can't be me, lucky, lucky me.

When Dad comes back from Mozambique he showers Mom with love and she's happy to see him. She makes his favourite meal and is on her best behaviour. This lasts for a few days and then the fear seeps back in. Dad becomes the wolf and we are all his sheep in beautiful clothing. I am still glowing with my love for Dale and this makes Dad furious.

So here we go …

'Candice, stop being rude. I'll kick you out of this house and take you to your real father,' says Dad.

'Whatever.'

'I'm warning you.'

'What do you want from me, Dad?'

'Get in the car now.'

In the car we go, windows closed and doors locked.

'Scream, Candice, scream like your life depends on it.'

'Why?'

'Do it. If you don't scream, you're going to live with your father.'

The thought of being dropped off at my father scares me. I don't know him anymore and my early memories of him don't want me to knock on his door.

'But Dad, I can't …'

'Scream!'

'Aaahhh …' I whisper.

'Louder.'

'Aaaahhh …'

'Scream your anger out.'

'I can't, I can't scream.'

'Ahh …'

'… Dad, please …'

'Again, scream …'

'Dad! … AAAHHHHH!'

'Good, let's go home and don't ever behave like a hooligan again.'

I'm silent, exhausted, hot and sweaty. I've run a marathon and crossed the finishing line. I need fluid and half-time oranges.

'I love you, Candice.'

Oh good, my fucking medal.

'Let's go home. No more nonsense, no more attitude.'

So home we go, to my big home, filled with books, furniture, paintings, love, clothes, abuse, pots, food, hate, beds and sisters.

I can't tell Dale, I can't tell Mom and I can't tell my sisters. When it comes to talking about my dad, my tongue feels cut out of my mouth, my throat closes and I have no words to tell the truth. There is no way out of my situation, I'm stuck for now. Dad has me in his grip and there is nothing I can do. Talking hurts people; the truth breaks people. If chaos were to come pouring out of my mouth, what would happen afterwards?

Thirteen comes with changes. Unwelcome blood flows between my legs and I am given a tampon by my mom. She teaches me to put it inside my never-before-touched vagina.

I'm thirteen and this is the first 'woman day' of the rest of my life.

I get a heavy flow for someone so small and also get heavy moods. My hips are taking on a new shape and they dance even when I'm not moving.

I'm not sure about this body change; it's sexy, but I'm not ready to grow into a woman and have extra-large boobs and curves. Curves plus men equals sex, and I don't want that. I still like the simple things in life: kittens, strawberries and ice cream; of course, now that my hips have a swing, I'll only have one scoopful.

I'm hoping that my coming into womanhood will stop Dad from all his doings, in case I fall pregnant and have his child. Unfortunately, I fear that nothing stops a man with a cause.

Acting is still a big part of my life. I love performing and the freedom of being someone else, leaving my body, leaving Candice Derman, becoming a strong girl, a girl who loves without fear.

Dale sees that girl inside of me. He thinks I'm special, with something to offer the world. I like the girl that Dale sees and I'll act her until I become her. When we are together, I pretend it's a lifetime and this helps me during the times when I am not with Dale.

INDESCRIBABLE

My short list of what I love at thirteen:

1. *Dale.*
2. *Dale.*
3. *Dale.*
4. *Dale.*

fourteen

Dale is dead.

Silence. I've just got out the bath.

'Candice, Dale's dead. He died in a car accident.'

I stand there dripping, with a towel around me to hide my grown-up bits. I'm staring into Gran's face, all fat, pink and wrinkled. Her mouth is moving but I hear nothing. I'm dead to what she is saying.

I walk away and go back into the bathroom. I feel my heart fall. It falls to my feet. I lose my balance and sit on the edge of the bath. I can't hear myself breathing. I feel nothing. I wait. I sit. Nothing. My heart has fallen from me and I am numb.

Death has entered my own body.

Dale's dead. He's never coming to visit me, never going to look at me, never coming back. Dale, my Dale. Dead. Gone.

Everyone is in Mozambique. I'm at home with Gran and a friend who is sleeping over. We were going to watch videos all night, but now I have to tell her to leave, to go home and leave me to my nothingness. Part of me wants her to stay with me, watch videos, eat popcorn and pretend nothing has changed.

'You need to go home.'

'Why?'

'Dale's dead.'

'What? When? Oh, my G-d, are you okay?'

'I need to be alone.'

'Are you sure, can't I stay?'

My boyfriend is dead. Dale, my Dale. The Dale who wiped away my dirt and made me clean.

'No really, thanks, I need to be alone.'

She leaves with tears in her eyes and mouths, 'I'm sorry.'

I'm alone now and I take out all the letters that Dale and I wrote to each other; our letters of love, explanation, apology. Please, please let this not be true. I cry, but my tears are short and sharp. Different thoughts move past each other so quickly in my head. I can't make sense of the suddenness of his death, of never seeing Dale again.

I want to vomit, I want to scream, I want to die. My heart is beating so fast, so hard.

I'm in my bed in my pink pyjamas, in my fucking pink bedroom, and my boyfriend is dead. I try to cry but nothing comes. My body starts doing what it does best, alienating me, cutting me off from reality. Thoughts leave me, I become empty and sleep summons me.

The days that follow are a blur: the memorial service, the sleepovers at his mom's, and the cries out loud in pain.

I'm confused, I can't think straight, I don't feel grounded or part of this earth.

I've got to get out of here, away from school, away from my memories and away from my family. My family returns from Mozambique, except for Dad. I am happy to see them but their love doesn't feel enough, it doesn't stitch up my gaping wound, so I pack my bags and leave for Mozambique.

I love Mozambique: the sea air, the people, the freedom and the long sunny days that turn my skin from sad olive into a beautiful brown. I feel happy in this post-war country, broken and penniless, and I embrace every pothole.

I arrive hoping to receive love from my dad. I need him to look after me, take away my pain, make me feel safe. I'm praying he holds me and doesn't have sex with me. I'm praying he will let me cry in his arms and not touch my privates. I'm praying, praying hard. I'm praying because right now I need him to be my dad.

'I'm so sorry about Dale.'

'Thanks Dad.'

'We will have a special few days, I will look after you.'

I take my bags to the spare room with the single bed. I am happy to be away from everyone in Johannesburg and I feel better.

Dad comes up the stairs.

'Don't be silly, sleep with me. We'll be a regular husband and wife.'

Regular? I am fourteen. Dad's forty-two or some-thing, so what's so regular?

Abused teenagers can be so stupid; what did I ex-pect? Why do I forget so quickly? Why do I want love from my devil? Do I need to feel pain because I've stopped feeling?

'Dad, please can I sleep in this room?'

'Candice, you came to see me because you wanted to be with me.'

'But Dad ...'

'No buts.'

Oh my G-d, Candice, what have you done? You've walked into this, you dirty slut. This is what you wanted. Your boyfriend is dead and your father is going to fuck you. Oh my G-d, Candice, who are you?

I can't answer my questions. They are all too over-whelming and I'm too tired to fight the bitch that lives within me.

Dad and I go out for dinner with some of his col-leagues. He's proud of me and shows me off. We go home, he's still proud of me, still shows me off. He drinks more wine and I go to bed early hoping he'll let me sleep. What's the chance?

I go upstairs and change into my summer pyjamas: shorts and a T-shirt with hearts on it. I laugh at them, at the fact that I have no heart myself but so many hearts on my pyjamas. I hope to fall asleep quickly. If I do, Dad will find his daughter in a foetal position and leave her to her dark dreams. But I know I can't fall asleep; my head is filled with murky thoughts, thoughts of death and thoughts of loss. My thoughts open the door to fear and I lie in bed, finding no solace in sleep.

I ask many 'why' questions. Why me? Why Dale? I'm restless and fear creeps deep into my body. I recognise fear. It is small with curly dark hair and blue eyes; it burns your stomach and causes aches and pains; it takes all the light away and brings in the darkness. I am no longer Candice Derman, I am fear.

I can hear Dad walking up the stairs. I pretend I'm asleep and quiet my breathing. He walks into the bedroom and I smell cigarettes, wine, and I smell desire coming out of him.

Dad strips down to his pubic bone. I'm not facing him but I know his thing is hard as stone. It's not going to go down until his blood pressure is released and since I'm the only nurse available, I'm the one who will have to relieve the pressure.

He lies next to me.

'Are you sleeping?'

I don't respond, he comes closer.

'Are you sleeping?'

I groan to let him know I'm in deep sleep. His smoky hands begin touching my hearts, then they move under the hearts and visit my soon-to-be hairy fanny. He opens my legs, I try to be stiff but I am as flexible as a cat, as loose as a rag doll. He turns me over with so much ease.

'Now you're awake.'

I guess I am.

'I love you, I love you so much.'

Hard and horny Daddy loves me.

'Don't worry, Candice, G-d understands.'

Dale, come and get me, take me away with you, you can leave a note: 'She deserved more', or 'Love is not about hurting', or maybe best of all, 'Candice has left the building, so fuck off!'

Dale doesn't arrive, the ceiling doesn't open up and show me the stars, so the next best thing is my imagination.

Dad enters me, moaning. He's moving up and down, licking my neck, touching my breasts. I close my eyes and I leave Dad and me alone and go to visit Dale, or at least I try. I'm floating above us; I see my moaning father and my lifeless body, I watch myself. I turn around and face the ceiling and go through it. I see the night, the stars and the perfectly clear dark sky. I float and look and wonder what it must be like to be an angel. I hear birds calling and dogs barking.

I keep getting pulled back into the room. I am holding on or trying to, I don't want to go back, I want to leave him but I am falling, falling fast.

I hear Dad groaning, I hear my silence. No, please, please I'm not ready to go back. I haven't seen Dale yet, please, but I arrive back in my lifeless body with a crash.

Damn, I hate it here.

Dad's about to come. He doesn't come inside me anymore now that I have my periods. He wouldn't risk me falling pregnant. Quickly he leaves my internal body and explodes on my external one. He's left my hearts pyjama top on so his cum is soaked into the hearts and not on me, lucky me.

I miss Dale, his smell, his lanky body and his freckles. I miss myself with Dale; I liked who I was and I wonder if I'll ever be happy again.

I fall asleep quickly, a deep sleep. Dale comes to me in a dream and I know he is looking out for me. I never told Dale about Dad, but now I guess he knows and this brings me comfort.

The next few days in Mozambique pass slowly; every day is much the same: sleep, eat, go to work with Dad, sit around, read, feel sad and feel lonely.

Dad has sex with me once or twice a day, but I don't care right now; I am tired of my tears, of fighting with myself, of feeling broken. He can have my body, poke wherever he wants to, lick, suck, pinch and bite any part of me. I am not my body, I am not my vagina, my breasts, my toes or my nose.

Since the dream, a numb calmness has come over me and deep down I feel strangely strong. I know he can't really have me, not my soul. I know this will pass and I will be living my own life in a place of hope, love, healing and imagination. I know, because I have had so many good days in between the bad, and even in my darkest moments I eventually fly to the light. And I know because there is no other way for me.

Dad can drown me and bang my head on the table, he can curse and shout, but he has nothing of me. Not the Candice that Dale showed me, not the Candice I'll one day become. I'm not a victim. There is more to me than this pain, this raw rubbing. I am more than all the moments Dad has taken from me.

This anaesthetised strength eases the pain. Tomorrow I might feel different, maybe I'll be crazy sad, but today I am okay. So, Joe di Bivar, you don't know this, no one does, but I've signed a contract with myself that, no matter how dark my life is now, one day I will be happy. I will find love and you will be a distant memory.

Perhaps I signed this contract with G-d before I arrived in Mozambique, maybe I signed it today, but however it came about, I know there will be an out.

Dad uses me a lot this holiday. He does me every way, every angle, every moment and then it's time for us to go home.

My home is an empty shell full of crap. I am bitter and angry, but I am also fourteen, so in between the contract, the numbness, crossness and a bit of confusion, there is lots of play.

I start dating boys again, too quickly for anyone's liking, even my own, but I don't really care if they are judging me; I judge myself. Nothing is serious with anyone, but I have nothing better to do. If I stop, I will see that everything around me is rotting. I'm failing at school, life and being a good daughter. Luckily I have looks on my side, and Valentine's Day to reward me.

I arrive home with a bag full of goodies, cards, teddy bears and balloons. I'm a girl in demand and I feel good.

'Look what I got Dad.'

I turn the bag of goodies upside down and the cards fall to the floor.

They say: 'Be my Valentine', 'For someone special' and 'You're the one'.

I'm glowing with all the love and my cheeks are rosy pink from all the affirmation.

'What's all this?' Dad asks.

'They're my Valentine's cards,' I say, with a little apprehension. I know Dad isn't going to like the attention I'm getting.

'Boys only want you for one thing, Candice.'

My cheeks are still rosy and my enthusiasm at an all-time high.

'Whatever!'

'What did you say?'

'Whatever!!!'

'Oh, so now you're a big deal. You think because you've got all these gifts and cards, you're something special.'

My glow is still visible but anger is setting in. Why does Dad always want to spoil my fun? I turn my back, not wanting to look at him, not wanting him to take away my high.

'Don't turn your back on me.'

I don't reply, I can't reply. What can I say?

Dad turns me around, grabs my arm and looks down at me, fury in his dark eyes.

'Don't ever turn your back on me again.'

I look at him defiantly. I want out, out of this so-called father-daughter relationship, out of his tight grip.

'Don't ever get too big for your boots, you hear me?' Dad is still holding on to me, shaking me, slapping me over and over.

Finally, he looks over at my cards of love. He gets down on the floor and starts tearing my cards into tiny pieces, one by one.

My cheeks are no longer flushed, my glow has faded and all love has gone. Dad tears up my cards, rips my teddies and pops my balloons, which drop to the floor, lifeless.

'That will teach you. Now tidy this mess up.'

Dad leaves the room. One by one, I begin picking up the pieces with tears streaming down my face.

One moment I was loved, the next it was gone. I'm nothing more than my cards, all torn up. I look together but I'm not. I'm broken, pieces of me just rattling around inside my small frame.

Why doesn't Dad take me and really break me? Why does he leave me only a little bruised, intact on the outside but internally broken?

I gather all the rubbish and throw it in the bin. It shouldn't have meant so much to me. If I hadn't had the cards, none of this would have happened, so from this day on, I ban Valentine's Day: You want to love me? Make it every day.

The dark days are lasting longer and the kind Dad is harder to find. Business is not going well and I think Mom and Dad are in trouble financially. They argue a lot and Mom always ends up in tears with Dad always the triumphant winner. Mom later apologises and things go back to normal.

Dinner is served to our king: oxtail with roast potatoes, followed by mango pudding and ice cream. With everything laid out perfectly, we all sit and eat our feast. I look around the table; what a lovely lie. How did we get here?

I suck the oxtail bone and put the marrow on a piece of bread and thank G-d for the food, because a good meal always makes up for a bad day. I look at Dad and smile, Dad smiles back.

I HATE YOU. I smile, but my eyes have no expression. I hope he can see my hate. I am the Rambo of girls, that's me, although no one knows it. In some moments I believe I'm tough, in other moments I believe I'm weak. My life is a pendulum of emotions as I struggle to cope with Dad's Dr Jekyll and Mr Hyde.

I fail standard seven, which is not a surprise. I repeat the year not remembering anything I learned before. It's like the first time I've been in this class, the first time I'm learning all these subjects. Where was I for a whole year? What scares me is that no one asks why. I guess it's easier to believe I'm slow, naughty and conceited. Imagine thinking her dad might be a paedophile and the only learning she is doing is survival training.

Almost seven years have gone by and nothing has eased, other than during the times when he is away. Even then he has started to call and ask if I'm missing him, missing what we do. Somehow he forces a 'yes' out of me; even though he is so far away, I'm still terrified of him.

'Do you miss me?'

Silence. 'Yes.'

'Do you miss my touching you?'

Silence. 'Yes.'

I want to vomit and all I can do is respond with a weak, sickly 'Yes'.

'Write me a letter. Tell me how bad.'

'Dad.'

'Come on, Candice, I hate being away from you. Do it for me.'

Silence.

'Okay. I'll get Mom on the line for you.'

'Love you.'

'Love you too, Dad,' abuser man.

FOURTEEN

My letter goes something like this:

Dear Dad, I miss you so much. I miss playing our games. See you soon. Love me.

I write it because he told me to, I write it because I think there is no way out, I write it because I'm scared not to, I write it because I don't know why I write it.

still
fourteen

I'm growing frustrated and angry. Everything feels like it's coming to a head, a pimple that needs to be squeezed. I am so alone, winded by life, dead but not. There is blood coursing through my veins, wet in my eyes and panic in my body.

Something is burning in me. I don't know why or where it is coming from but I want to meet my real dad. I don't care that my memories of him aren't packed with fun. I'm desperate, ready for him to deliver me from evil and save my soul. I'm not really sure how to handle the situation, because Mom hates Lionel and doesn't want to have anything to do with him. Loving him may mean I don't love her. Kim and I aren't close so I wouldn't discuss it with her and Jodi is on her own mission, so I choose to speak to Romy.

'Rome, I've been thinking.'

'Yah,' she is kind of ignoring me, studying for her history exam. Maybe Napoleon is much more interesting.

'It's a secret and I don't want you to tell anyone.'

She looks up at me; I manage to get more of her attention.

'A secret?'

'Yah, there is something I want to tell you, but you've got to promise not to tell anyone.' Now I have her full attention. Napoleon is out the door and history where it should be.

Romy looks concerned, I'm not sure why. Her golden locks around her angel face somehow look like they're dropping. Her beautiful electric green eyes start turning a dull, stained yellow. She stares at me. Silence. I'm worried, confused; what does she know? We stare at each other and I recognise her expression: a dark, sombre look. I reflect the same look back at her.

'Candice, what do you want to tell me?'

'Well …'

'Just tell me.'

'Okay, it's …'

'Has Joe done something to you?' There is terror in her voice.

What? Oh my G-d! Where did that come from? My heart feels like it's been punched, the air rushes from my lungs. I start to float.

'Has he touched you? Candice, I asked you a question.'

I can't answer. This is not where I was going, not what I wanted to face, not now, not ever. Get me out of here body.

'Candice!'

I can't answer her, I won't answer her, but some-how from deep inside my belly, from the back of my throat, a 'yes' forces open my tightly shut mouth. My evil body has deceived me. I wanted to leave but she has forced out the ugly truth.

'Yes.'

This voice is not mine; it's old and has kept a dark secret for a very long time.

It feels like the 'yes' echoes around us. Oh my G-d, how did that come out? A secret I've been carrying for a childhood eternity has just left my body. I'm stunned. I'm looking at Romy and Romy is looking back at me. There is a deathly silence.

'When did it start?'

I am a robot, dutifully answering her questions.

'Before Mom and Dad got married.'

'How often?'

'Nearly every day?'

'Has he done more than touch you?'

'Yes.'

'What?'

'You know.'

'No, I don't.'

'Rome, I can't really talk about this.'

'Candice, you have to.'

'He has sex with me.'

'Oh my G-d!'

Romy looks terrified and she starts to cry. Tears fall on her history notes and smudge her neat handwriting. We don't talk for what seems like hours. I'm so confused by this voice from deep inside that has escaped its jail, like a convict who breaks out and creates havoc. We sit paralysed, speechless. I've said too much and my world has been turned upside down. I'm spinning inside myself.

Romy and I sit for a long time. I keep looking at her slowly changing expressions. I wonder how I'm going to get out of here, how I'm going to escape the truth. Eventually we decide to go for a walk. We need to move our pain away, get some fresh air and walk awhile. We find ourselves sitting under a mulberry tree. She is full and green and dressed in all her spring wonder. I pick mulberries, we talk, sit, hold hands, hug and cry. I take out my Lip Ice and laugh, it's mulberry flavoured. Everything is so funny. This moment, our situation. Funny because it looks so pretty, two curly heads sitting under one of G-d's trees eating mulberries and chatting about the horror of abuse.

Romy tells me Dad's touched her down there. Nothing more but nothing less.

I explain how Dad has had sex with me for many years. I tell her about the blow jobs, the drowning, the fear. We talk so much and talking helps. It doesn't take away the rawness but it eases the pain.

'Candy, I'm so sorry.'

It starts to get dark and we walk home, to our house of evil. I feel too full of dirt and conversation and go to the toilet and vomit. Vomit mulberries and pain, secrets and cum, fear and loathing.

Romy tells me we have to tell Mom. This frightens me so much. How did it get to this? For years I lived a lie and now I am untangling this web of deceit and I am frightened. Dad's in Mozambique but he's coming home soon. I'm so confused, what have I done? I love him?

What's going to happen? He'll tell everyone I'm a liar. What's Mom going to do? What's she going to say? This is too much to bear. Dale's gone and soon Dad will be gone. Is this all my fault? Am I bad?

I'm sinking, sinking. This feeling is worse than Dad forcing himself on me. At least when Dad is on me I can escape. I taught my head to fly, but now there is no escape. I'm desperate and I don't know what to do with myself.

TICK. TICK. TICK.

I'm stuck; time passes so slowly.

TICK. TICK. TICK.

Romy tells me we'll tell Mommy tomorrow and goes to visit her boyfriend. She has somewhere to go, a shoulder to cry on, a safe place to hide. I am left alone with my ticking. My fragility is disabling.

TICK. TICK. TICK.

Maybe I should run away and then I won't have to face this. Maybe I should kill myself and all this will be over. Maybe.

TICK. TICK. TICK.

Mom comes home. Oh my G-d. She's just been to the hairdresser. I must hold back my tears. I stand in front of her and stare at the mom I love so much, the mom whose life is going to change in the blink of my eye. She looks perfect. Thick bob, heavy fringe, eye shadow dark and sexy. My mom, a modern-day Cleopatra. I am so sorry.

TICK. TICK. TICK.

'Your hair looks beautiful!' I put on a forced smile.

'You think so? I hate it.'

'Mom, it's perfect.'

Tomorrow she won't be thinking about her hair. Oh my G-d, I'm so sorry.

'What do you want for dinner?'

'Nothing, I'm not hungry, I'm going to bed.'

'So early, are you okay?'

'Yes, just tired.'

TICK. TICK. TICK.

Dad's been abusing me for years. How am I going to force those words out? How am I going to live afterwards?

'Sleep well, love you.'

'Love you, Mom.'

I walk along the passage, tears filling my eyes, down the stairs past Gran's bedroom, Romy's bedroom, Kim's bedroom and into mine. I am blinded by my sorrow. I shut the door, fall into my bed and tears come pouring out. I'm crying from exhaustion, crying for Dale, for my mom, for Dad and for what's to come. This is the most frightened I have ever been. I cry myself to sleep.

Romy returns home early. I can't eat. My body is shaking. I'm feeling weak. She tells Mom we have to talk.

'What about?' asks Mom.

'It's serious Mom, we can't talk here. Let's go for a drive.'

'You're worrying me, Romy.'

'Mom, just wait.'

We all get into our Kombi and drive to the park a few minutes away from the house. I am still shaking. Nausea overwhelms me and I think I'm going to faint. My mom switches off the engine and turns to face us.

Everything is about to change. Please G-d, protect my mom.

Romy starts, 'Joc's been having sex with Candice.'

Mommy goes white and the pretty olive colour drains from her face. Shock. Please faint, please faint, I beg my body, but Mom's asking questions and I'm forced to answer.

'When did it start?'

'When I was eight.'

'Oh my G-d! Why didn't you say anything?'

'I don't know, I just …'

Mom interrupts me.

'What are you talking about? Is it still going on? You mean Dad's been putting his penis inside you, inside your vagina?'

'Yes!' You fucking idiot, don't you think I know what I'm talking about?

Mom is hysterical. She's spitting tears and saliva. I watch a myriad different emotions pass through her. She's angry, sorry, shocked. I'm a rag doll. Every bit of power has left my body. Romy has been silenced. Wiped out.

Mom asks more questions. I answer. She gets louder, madder, more distorted. I watch the mascara leave her lashes and fall onto her cheeks, down her chin and onto her white shirt, which is now stained with black tears. This is my mom's new life: a life of black tears, tears of mascara, of desperation and loss. We are in the Kombi in our own world wanting so badly to escape each other, but we can't. We're here, facing our worst fears, facing each other.

It seems like a lifetime passes. We are still sitting pretty, pretty knocked out. This emotional crash has affected our heads, hearts and souls. No one will come to our rescue; no one will know that we have all been internally amputated. I don't recognise Romy or my mom, they have become broken pieces of the Kombi.

I had put what Dad was doing to me in a coffin that we lay in secretly together. Now the spotlight is on the story of my abuse, and I don't know what to do. I knew how to compartmentalise the different parts of me, but now I am a molten mass of Candice Derman, and I don't know if I'll ever find a part of me to love.

I am fourteen and I feel so old. This is a scary life, a scary, scary life.

'Mom, I'm so sorry.'

'It's not your fault Candice,' she whimpers.

Romy tells Mom what Dad did to her but by this time, Mom's almost flatlined.

We drive home, silenced by too many words. I'm hoping Mom will keep it quiet and not tell Dad. Not yet, anyway. I'm hoping Mom will work out what we're going to do logically and silently.

What was I thinking?

When we get home, my mom wastes no time in telling Gran. Her severed heart has put her in motion, an angry rampage. Her silence is over and the war has begun. Abuse is all she can see and I'm now an outline, not her daughter.

I run to my room to escape more changing expressions, more horror written on everyone's face. The madness I feel is extreme. I want to be in a boxing ring beating up my opponent; I want to be in hospital on a drip; I want my mom to hold me and tell me it's all going to be okay, but it won't, it never will be.

I hear my gran shouting, 'Oh my Lord Jesus ...' and wonder where the hell this Lord Jesus is right now. I shut my eyes and imagine Dale. What could have been, what should have been. I keep my eyes shut, shut tight and I pray to the universe. Please G-d, save me from this, from what I'm going to have to face.

I'm so tired and eventually surrender to my sadness. My tears dry, numbness protects me and slowly I fall asleep. Thank you sadness for helping me to sleep.

The next morning I wake up and get ready for school. Panties, uniform, socks and shoes. I'm shell-shocked by what happened last night. I figure doing what I normally do is the best way to face the world. I'm afraid to leave my room and face my family, see Mommy's face, Romy's nervous hands and hear Gran's 'Oh my Lord Jesus' sayings. None of them can save themselves or me.

I force myself to put one foot in front of the other and leave my room, walk into the house of echoes, past the bedrooms, up the stairs, and into the kitchen.

Mommy's dressed to perfection, hair and make-up in strategic place. She's pacing up and down the kitchen. Her tight top shows her ample cleavage, and hot jeans and stilettos only a catwalk model could wear complete her statement. There is a wall between us, a continent, a universe. I wonder if she blames me? There is no comfort in the fact that Mom believes me; the truth has crushed my family's foundation. We can participate in life, look like part of the human race, but today we are different, today our story has changed. Mommy's fantasy has evaporated, her husband is a bad man, her hope has vanished and it is entirely my fault. I want to collapse in on myself.

'Let's go … I'm going to drop you off at school and go to see the psychologist. I'm not sure how to handle this situation.'

'Okay.'

Gran hasn't come out of her room and I'm grateful for that. Perhaps she's still praying to G-d and maybe he will provide her with the answers I need.

So here I am at school, in maths class. Staring at the blackboard and watching Mrs Engelbrecht scribble numbers in chalk. I watch the black turn to white and see the numbers turn into letters. They say CANDICE DERMAN + ABUSE = SLUT.

My head leaves the classroom of Candice the slut and takes me to a better place. I use my technique of flowing away from the present. This place is far more peaceful. Good and evil don't exist here, just the quiet of nothingness. I slip further away. Maybe this is how I'll be able to heal myself in time: to float into the peace of quiet, knowing there is another life away from guilt and splattered pieces of heart. The bell rings for break and brings me back to the chalk that states the obvious about me.

Break comes and goes and I do what I do best. Chat to my friends, flirt with boys, and think of 101 ways to commit suicide. I'm in and out of the past, present and future. I've lost my place in the world. Like a bird with no nest, a lamp with no light bulb or bubblegum ice cream without the gum. The day is long. English class seems like I am learning a new language, maths makes me feel like I am an alien who has just landed, and the crumbs on my blazer show that food is my hidden solace.

Eventually the school day ends. Mom arrives in her aqua Porsche, with her aqua eyes. Mom doesn't deserve this lie of a life: she loves life, it is her playground. She is good at living her fairy tale, but her greatest flaw is forgetting that along the way fairy tales often get scary and nasty. I don't blame her for living in her chocolate box fantasy; I mean, who wouldn't want that?

I get into the car. Mom informs me of the proceedings for the day.

1. *See the psychologist.*
2. *Make a statement to the police.*
3. *Go to the government gynaecologist. (I guess they want to see what's up there in the land of my vagina.)*

Sounds nice.

I bite into my cheese pie and wonder what's to become of me. I try to make a list of all the things I love at fourteen:

1. *... ... blank*

I just eat the pie and long for my eighteenth birthday to come. We arrive at the psychologist's office. He starts asking me questions. I make a quick mental list of all the places I don't want to be:

1. *Home.*
2. *School.*
3. *In the car with Mom.*
4. *In the psychologist's office.*

'Hi Candice, my name is Dr Tillbury'

'Hi.' I've got nothing to say to this man.

'Your mom told me what your dad's been doing to you and I want to know how you're feeling.'

How the fuck do you think I'm feeling, mother-fucker?

'… mmmmnnn, I don't know, I'm confused.'

'That's understandable.'

Silence …

He speaks again: 'Your mom loves you very much, and this is going to be a very difficult time for all of you …'

You think …?

He's waiting for me to say something. I hate it here, I hate it here, I hate it here. I keep repeating these words in my head like a stuck record. He breaks my inner repetition with more meaningless words.

'We'll set up another meeting, in case you want to talk. In the meantime, you must tell the police everything you remember.'

'Okay.' Wow, that was life-changing. Thanks Mr Mother Fucker! You solved my life's problems in ten minutes.

We jump into the car again. Off to the police station we go. Mom and I don't speak to each other. We arrive after our long, non-talking journey, get out of the car and walk into the police station.

An Afrikaans man comes out to meet us.

'Young lady, please follow me. Madam, please wait here.'

I add the police station to my mental list of places I don't want to be.

I follow him and don't turn back to look at my mom. Oh my G-d, will he cuff me, put me in jail, blame me for everything, tell me I'm a terrible, terrible person?

'Sit over here,' he says.

I sit in a big chair that dwarfs me. He moves to sit at the opposite side of his desk. There are papers sprawled across it, pictures of babies and young people with bruises and burns. I feel sorry for them and I am comforted that Dad never burnt me with his cigarettes or broke my bones.

'So Candice, I have to take a statement from you. You must talk slowly and tell me everything. I have to ask questions that will be difficult to answer and I am sorry.'

His office smells smoky. The windows are closed and I'm thinking, please open your damn windows. The walls are covered with slogans: 'Stop abuse', 'Speak now', and posters of children with faces smudged with tears and women with black eyes.

This is a very bad world.

'Let's start. Tell me when you need a break.'

I already need a fucking break.

There are tissues perfectly positioned next to me on the desk. They're a bit dusty, as if there has been no child brave enough to cry in front of this Mr Policeman.

I look at him; I look through him; I want to get up and run, run out of his office, out of the building and onto the street. I want to run to another continent. Leave myself behind, wave me away and say goodbye to the abused me. But I just look at him. I can't speak, I feel stuck like a person with locked-in syndrome.

I sit and I wait; he sits and waits.

Eventually I get feeling in my body, like I've been plugged into a socket and a current is surging through me. My body forces my sob story out of me again.

I'm feeling cynical and old, vulnerable and young. I talk and tell him where, how, when it started and on what days. I want to cry but I hold back my tears. I fight them. I know I'll punish myself if they fall. I continue telling him my story, cold and impersonal, telling my story as if it hasn't had a major impact on my life and shaped my fourteen years. He listens, writes in a scrawl and asks questions. He takes a peppermint and sucks on it. I wonder why he doesn't offer me one. I could do with a peppermint.

We finish late. The gynaecologist will have to wait until tomorrow. He pats me on the shoulder.

'Well done, you did good.'

'Thanks.'

He walks me back to reception. I notice him eye-balling my mom. I'm sure he's thinking, 'That's one sexy momma, why on earth did the dad need to go near the kid?'

I'm not sure how I get through the next few hours. Mom cries to her friends on the phone as tears spill down her made-up rosy cheeks. Gran carries on praying but G-d's not helping. Jodi and Kim have left the building and Romy and I just hold on to each other and try to survive the night.

'Candy, I love you so much.'

'I love you too, Rome.'

Morning arrives. I have to miss school and Romy has decided to come to the gynaecologist with me. I add the gynaecologist to my mental list of places I don't want to be. The hospital is ugly, a perfectly cold, sterile environment. No welcome, just open your legs and enjoy the ride. We walk through the icy corridors and into an ugly office. I am so glad Romy is with me.

'Put this gown on and take off your clothes and underwear. I'll be back in a few minutes,' says the nurse who is waiting for me.

Three older women return. My legs are opened up. One woman feels inside. The other woman takes close-up pictures of my vagina with a really large camera, and the third one is there, just because. Maybe she is going to be a nurse and she is learning. Just my luck to get a 'no-reason' nurse standing and staring at the opening of my few-pubic-hairs vagina. I wonder if she thinks it's a pretty one.

There is no positive to this situation, no gold star for being a survivor. I hate this so much. I hate these three women busying themselves in places they are not wanted. I lie there forcing myself to breathe, forcing myself to see further than the present, to find something worthwhile and good to hold on to.

I squeeze Romy's hand and think how much I love her. It's a big, huge, complete love. I capture this feeling, force the love into my heart and let it flow through me. Slowly the love grows, my breathing eases and it helps me get through this moment. And then I realise, in amongst this ugliness, with my legs wide open and people invading my vagina, that love is like medicine: it helps me heal. So I make a promise to myself that in this life I am going to love so hard that the pain subsides. I am going to love so hard that the bad dissolves into a small amount of blood in my body and that it won't own me. I am going to love so hard that I beat Joe and become a winner, a survivor. And I'll wear an internal sash that says, 'Lover of life'.

Fairy tales can be evil and messy along the way, but they always have happy endings, and I demand mine.

I smile at my thoughts and I am brought back to the present by the flash of the camera. I wonder if my vagina was smiling at the right moment. I give

Romy's hand another squeeze and her eyes a silent thank you. The photo shoot is over. They see Dad's penetrated me and they have their evidence. I don't get a sucker for good behaviour.

Panties on, clothes on and off we go back home.

Life just carries on. I eat my three meals a day, have some snacks and avoid my family's eyes, which is not difficult to do because they are avoiding mine. My sisters have boyfriends and this keeps them 'happily' occupied. Mom hasn't been able to get hold of Dad for days and we're not sure why. We don't know when he'll be coming back but we do know he will be heading home soon and I'm petrified.

I go to school and act as if everything is normal, which is easy because all I've got to do is continue failing.

Knowing the Devil is going to arrive any day now is at the back of all of our minds and that's a very dark, dark place to be.

The house has been struck by madness. There is a silent screaming taking place. I hear Mommy whispering on the telephone, words like bastard, psychopath, prick, paedophile. Other than that, it's the gloom of another perfect day.

We imagine Dad's arrival with every door that opens, every footstep, every knock, but still manage to continue with our various daily rituals. Mom's is the most interesting. Her morning begins with a naked face, bare for no one in the world to see. Slowly and

methodically it gets covered. A light base, heavy eye-
liner on both top and bottom lids, and many layers of
mascara. The first helps her to be the new Yvonne; the
second, third and fourth bring out the superhero in
her and make her blue eyes stand out. After the dark
layers of mascara, she moves to her lips: a passionate
pink liner with an extra passionate dollop of gloss. My
mom's nearly finished, except for her perfect bobbed
hair with a heavy fringe that has to be brushed.

She then runs a bath, the final part of her ritual.
Bubbles foam from her favourite bubble bath, Badedas.
The smell wafts from the bath and fills the bathroom
with a rich, clean elegance. I love this green, forest smell.
Even now with all my inner turmoil I can breathe in
deeply and enjoy the feeling of peace this smell brings.
My mom gets into the bath, lies back and sighs. A sigh
of relief. A moment that belongs to her. I watch her
body underneath the bubbles, breathing, holding and
exhaling. I watch her body thanking her for slowing
down and continuing with her morning ritual.

I look at my mom's face, the made-up one, the
cold one that hides all her hurt, all her anger and all
her fear, and I notice she has gone floating somewhere
behind the mask, somewhere under the bubbles.
I want to envelop my mother in love but all I can
do is stare. Our love is complicated. It comes with
secrets and lies, protection, pride, sadness and pain. I
button up my school shirt and turn my face towards
the mirror.

I am no longer looking at my mother's superhero face but instead I am staring at my own made-up face. I don't need make-up to change me; I just need to change my expressions. If I lift my turning-down lips, make them smile at the corners, I look sweet, innocent, even untouched, perhaps. If I put my hair in a banana clip and let my locks fall, I could pass for a princess. If I open my eyes wide enough and force a sparkle, I look almost childlike.

My mom and I are the same. She dresses up with her mask; I dress up with 101 expressions of 'I'm so fucking happy, don't you want to be me?' We're both winning the war by hiding what we really feel and showing the razzle and dazzle of utter success. These lies should win us both Oscars. People see the external me: she is missing Dale but coping so well; shame, she is sweet but a little dim; she really knows how to have a good time. But if I peeled away my 101 expressions and told my truth, it would go something like this: I'm petrified of life, scared of death, and I live in fear of Dad's arrival. Fear is a weak word for such an underground feeling; it should be illegal to feel this afraid.

I'm lost.

I'm lonely.

I'm angry.

I'm numb.

I'm confused.

This is my truth.

With Dale gone, Dad nowhere to be found and with no one to talk to, I'm living a very vacant life. I should rent out my body and let some deserving person take me over for a while.

Mommy's going out a lot at night with her friends, keeping herself busy so as not to go mad and blow her pretty brains out. I wish I could go out, keep myself busy. My pink bedroom feels like it's caving in on me and I have to escape or I'll suffocate.

It's raining so hard outside, thunder that deafens, lightning that shoots electric fear. I run out of my room, mirroring my eight-year-old self, and sneak into my mom's bed. The night is filled with fury and I toss and turn. I try to find a comfortable spot, but no such luck; after all, this is the bed where it all began, in the early hours of the morning, when Joe's fingers did the talking. I am immobilised with fear, I can't stop the thunder in my head, the chatter of madness, or the chatter of my teeth.

I get out of the bed and run to Romy's room. I snuggle up next to her, so close her breath is on my shoulder. I have a bad feeling. The rain is so fucking hard. I get even closer to Romy; my palms are wet with anticipation and subconscious knowing.

The knock comes loud and clear. It's as if the thunder, lightning and rain have paused to give the knock greater emphasis. Romy and I are silenced; we know it's the dark man. What the fuck are we going to do?

The brass knocker echoes. Knock, knock, knock.

We hear his mom screaming at him, screaming for G-d to help.

'Lord Jesus, Lord Jesus.'

Romy and I are shivering in the bed like two little mice with nowhere to hide. We have eaten the poison and are just waiting to die, waiting for our grim reaper to come and fetch us.

More screaming in tongues, screaming at Joe, 'My son, my son, go away.'

The thunder is so angry, maybe it's on our side.

Romy and I, eyes wide open, terrified, get out of the bed and run to Jodi's bedroom.

Dad shouts questions, Gran tries not to answer and speaks to Jesus instead. More tongue talk. Not sure what is being said, only G-d knows.

Eventually English, 'How could you?'

'What are you talking about, Mom?'

'You know, with Candice?'

'Just let me in.'

'I can't, go away.'

Long talks to Jesus.

Jodi is sitting up in bed. None of us can speak, we're listening to the Devil and his mother.

'What about Candice?'

'You slept with her … You touched Romy.'

'Just let me into my house, they are lying.'

'No, no, no … Go away.'

Dad is here and he's coming to get me. Maybe he will kill us all. I'm terrified, shivering takes a hold of my body.

'No, no, no … Go away.'

Tears, thunder, lightning.

We are all staring at the empty space that Gran and Dad's voices seem to occupy in the room.

Eventually Gran relents and lets Dad in. I count to myself: one, two, three … Trying to calm down, but nothing can stop my terror. He storms downstairs as angry as the weather, following our whispers and whimpers to Jodi's bedroom. No time for prayer, I am going to have to face this man, this waking nightmare.

He starts ranting at Romy

'You, you …,' he's stuck for words.

He's big and ugly but at the same time still just looks like Dad.

He spits out the words, 'How could you?'

I'm sitting on the bed next to Jodi; Romy's standing in the corner looking thinner than usual. I guess we're all looking thinner. At any other moment I might have liked the skinny me, but right now the thought does not cross my mind. Dad doesn't look at me; he's pretending I'm not there.

'What are you trying to do, put another nail in my coffin?' He's huffing and puffing and wants to blow the house down.

'Why are you doing this to me?'

Romy is shaking, she's at her most scared and I feel a surge of my most angry self. I don't know where my strength is coming from: I would beat him up if I could.

'Get out!' I shout at this man I once loved, this man I call Dad. 'Get out of our lives, that's what we want, for you to go. We hate you.'

My strength is leaving. Candice the weak is returning.

In the midst of all this turmoil superwoman arrives. Dry under her umbrella, perfect under her mask, cold and hard with the help of her raw wounds. She tells her husband to follow her. He does. The screaming begins. Superwoman walks up and down, the sound of her six-inch heels echoing as they punch the floor.

Romy runs out of the room and locks herself in her bedroom. Jodi and I stare into the thick empty space that still carries the heavy, smoky aura of Dad.

Jodi lifts herself from the draining silence and suggests we phone Dr Tillbury. Kim appears from her bedroom, eyes large and lost. The three of us march out into the pouring rain and into Dad's office. They think it's a good idea to phone from there so as not to arouse suspicion. Not that we would have: Supermom has Dad in her web and is trying to eat him alive.

The rain is a welcome relief, it's hard and angry and it calms my beating heart. I wish I could become one of the raindrops, water that will eventually disappear.

'How could you?!' Mom screeches.

'They're lying, Yvonne.'

'You're the liar. Who are you? Fucking bastard. I hate you.'

This is what I have done. I should have waited until I was eighteen and run away. No one would have known. I could have spared them all this pain. Mom should just as well be screaming the same words at me.

'Who are you? Fucking bitch. I hate you.'

Dr Tillbury arrives. The time between the phone call, the thunder, Mom's screaming and his arrival is a blur. He tells Jodi to keep everyone calm. Fucking hell, he's a fucking genius.

'Joe, calm down,' Dr Tillbury says.

'How dare you tell me to calm down? They're lying, they're trying to break up my marriage. I don't know why they would lie like this.'

Mom rants, 'I swear, I'll kill you.' I have never seen her in such a tirade.

'That's enough. Everyone listen to me, we all need to calm down and think rationally. We can sort this out. Joe, I suggest that you sleep at a hotel tonight, and you and Yvonne can meet in my office first thing tomorrow morning.'

A deathly silence comes over the room and all of a sudden the wolf gives up. Dad agrees to Dr Tillbury's request and leaves with his tail between his legs.

Dr Tillbury disrupts the zombie state my mom, sisters and I have slipped into. 'I have to go. Please all try to look after yourselves tonight. I'll make sure that everything is okay.'

He'll make sure everything is okay? Who does he think he is? Not even G-d can make this okay.

Kim and Jodi go back to bed; Mommy goes to bath; Gran prays to Lord Jesus; and I am left alone to think of my options.

1.   *Slit my wrists.*
2.   *Hang myself with a belt.*
3.   *Take pills.*
4.   *Run away.*
5.   *Eat a toasted sandwich.*
6.   *Watch TV.*
7.   *Go and lie in Mommy's bed and forget the world just caved in.*

We have a winner! Option seven.

I pretend I'm sleeping when Mommy comes to bed. She slips in close to me and all I can hear is her uneven breathing. I wish she would say something to me, something kind and caring, but she is incapable of softening her rigid, angry body, incapable of using untrue words of comfort. We can't fall asleep and we can't talk to each other; we are just trying to breathe, trying to live through this frightful night.

G-d really forgot to give parents a seventh sense so that they could see into their children's hearts.

My list of how I think my mom should be looking after me:

1.   *Tell me she loves me and that everything is going to be okay.*

122

2. *Create happy moments.*
3. *Remember I'm the child.*
4. *Take me to the movies.*
5. *Talk to me about the abuse.*
6. *Talk to me about other things.*
7. *Force a fucking smile.*

Eventually I fall asleep. My body forces me into another world and before I know it, it's morning and I have survived the worst day of my life.

Up on my worst day list:

1. *Dale's death.*
2. *The first time Dad touched me.*
3. *Being drowned.*
4. *Dad fucking me.*
5. *Mom finding out the truth.*
6. *Dad's arrival.*

I go to school, or at least my body does. I'm a zombie but no one picks up on this. My daily report reads, 'Candice was very well behaved today.' Maybe I'll always need darkness to keep me on the straight and narrow.

Mom is an hour late to pick me up from school and as I wait, sitting on the ground throwing stones onto the street, I wonder what will happen to us, how my family will survive this and if Dad will kill me.

Finally I see the Porsche. I get up, dust off the back of my skirt and get into the car.

'Hi,' I say.

'It was the worst morning of my life. The police arrested Joe, they should lock him up and throw away the key, but knowing him he will make bail,' vomits out my mom.

Blah, blah, blah. I hear my mom talking but I have tuned her out. The last thing I hear her say is she can't believe that this has happened to her, and I'm wondering if she's forgotten that it happened to me.

I am fourteen going on fifteen. I have lost my boyfriend, my dad and my virginity. The reflection I see when I look in the mirror is confusing. I'm an average teenager with above-average assets, perfectly round breasts, a flat tummy and olive skin, but my internal reflection is old and grey. I carry knowledge beyond my years and my above-average ass has been touched too many times. If I look in the mirror for too long, I fall inside me and lose myself, and by the time I've finished staring, I've become a grain of sand.

No one is there for me and I resent everyone I love. My sisters are silent witnesses and my mom just puts one foot in front of the other. I need help, and I need it fast. I start reading a book called *Letters to Judy* by Judy Blume. Teenagers write to her about all their problems. I can't put this book down. I'm surprised and comforted knowing that I'm not the only girl walking around broken and beaten by life. I am also shocked that there are so many me's out there. Judy's book becomes my confidante and even though she doesn't know me, I feel she understands. I've already decided it's going to be up to me to heal myself, but reading about other teenage lives eases my inner isolation and helps me move forward.

There is a newspaper lying on my mom's bed. It is open on page three: *Jose de Bivar* (how nice of them to use his full name) *has been accused of repeatedly raping his step-daughter*. My name has not been mentioned. I'm sure no one I know would have read this sad tale and if they did, they wouldn't know that I'm the unfortunate stepdaughter.

I'm still thrown. Seeing it in writing makes it all seem so real, makes the abuse more tangible. I have this small clipping; like a tattooed Holocaust survivor, this is my proof. I have lived through this.

I really thought my first newspaper article would be about Candice Derman, the talented young actress hitting the theatre scene. Just my luck, I'm now known as the faceless, nameless, abused girl.

My day will come. I feel it in my veins, in my spirit, and this picks me up, fills my being and makes me really hungry for some bubblegum ice cream. Today I'm not watching my weight. I want to lick the cold stuff and feel like a normal teenager with an ice cream craving.

My list of what's normal for me:

1. *Go to school.*
2. *Live in fear.*

3. *Try to remember the good parts of me.*
4. *Lie to my friends.*
5. *Daily dreams, prayers and wishes that one day my family and I will be okay.*

My mom was right, Joe did get bail, only R2000. Some ex-girlfriend paid for him. Nice woman. She must really like bad men who like young girls. I hate her, I hate her. Now he is walking and talking, eating and laughing, living and sleeping, while me and my family are sleepwalking and not talking, struggling to eat and not laughing, living in a coma and never sleeping.

When a family has been stung by the horror of abuse, there is an allergic reaction. Mouths close and minds seize up; no one can talk about it and no one can forget about it. Everyone just has to carry on living, living dead.

Thank goodness my friends don't know. They talk about boys, movies and actors; they worry about teachers and passing exams. It's a wonderful relief. I'll never tell them about my sordid life of a large penis and a small vagina. They will never know.

My days consist of school, then seeing the psychologist and the prosecutor. These have become my after-school activities. They are getting me ready for the day I have to stand up in court and tell the judge my sad tale. I'm not sure why Romy doesn't have to talk about Dad's misguided fingers and I'm not going to ask. The more I avoid conversations about Dad's manhandling, the better it is for my family and me. It is so much easier living a life of avoidance.

I hate all the buildings I have to be in. School is so ugly: brown desks and chairs, dirty, off-white walls and long corridors. My psychologist's office is not much better: the walls are crisp white but the décor is cold and the room sparse.

The worst building is the court: brick, grey, dark and depressing, with wood that has creaked and cracked over the years, greeting murderers, sex offenders, robbers, paedophiles and victims with wet eyes.

While I'm being coached and questioned by the prosecutor I can't help wondering why these buildings have to be so goddamn ugly. Why can't they repaint, bring in some colour and light? They should create a safe room for all the unsafe hearts and minds.

'Candice, are you okay? You seem so far away. Do you want to talk about anything?'

'No, I'm fine.' I really want to suggest a new coat of paint. Maybe they could bring in a palette of blues and greens, pretty landscape paintings or fresh flowers.

My mind drifts in and out of redecorating the office and hearing the prosecutor talk to me about my own life, asking questions. When? How often? When was the last time?

I think back to the last time, Dad towering over me, handsome, overweight and strong, 'I love you, Candice.'

Those were my dad's words. Words I wanted to hear so often, like a starving child in Ethiopia. My greed to be loved was enormous; I wanted to eat up Dad's love. I think about him picking me up and starting to tongue me, rough, kissing me like a cannibal, wanting to eat my body. I remember him throwing me on the bed, greed in his eyes, pulling off my pants and then my panties, cradling my breasts over my T-shirt. I think about him stumbling out of his trousers and taking off my T-shirt and bra, my nipples erect, deceiving me and him. I remember the smell of his nakedness, his hard penis pushing inside me. We had done this so many times before. Hundreds? Thousands? Who's counting? I would never get used to it.

I remember him hurting me, holding my breasts too tight and moving in and out too fast. I remember waiting for him to come, for the end, I remember. Little did I know that this would be the end, the end of Dad forcing me to become his little woman, of being his sex toy, of being his daughter, of Dad saying, 'I love you', the end of ever talking to Dad again. Had I known, would I have behaved differently? Could I have asked, 'Why Dad?' Would he have answered, 'Because I can't help myself, I love you and I am sorry.' Would I have forgiven him? Do I forgive him? I don't think in these terms. The best way I can move forward is not to think of Dad with kindness, not to love him, but to hate him; he is not milk and honey, he is battery acid.

I leave the prosecutor's office bewildered and shell-shocked. Things have moved too quickly, from a secret I have carried deep within the hidden parts of me, to everyone knowing. My life has been smashed into pieces and I have no idea how to put it back together again.

'How did it go?'

'I don't want to talk about it, Mom.'

'Fine.'

Silence, an unbearable silence. I try not to look at her. I don't want to see the depth of sadness in her eyes. I look straight in front of me, at nothing.

The drive home takes about fifteen minutes, a lifetime. I age in those fifteen minutes; I become weathered, depleted and old. I am fourteen and I am old. I have to learn to forgive myself, learn to love myself. If I don't, sadness will eat away at my core and I will begin to rot.

Home has become a house of horrors, a place that holds the past in its clutches. My bedroom, with its sickly pink theme, makes me want to vomit. I hate the innocence of this room. A lie. I see my mom's bedroom, Dad's love den. So many times he's taken me in their bed, in the jacuzzi, a place to touch my privates, the pool, a quick, wet, easy place to slip inside of me, or a place to drown me. I've been had on every stool, couch and chair. No room lets me escape my past, every room carries the heaviness of my yesteryears.

The phone rings. Mom answers. I watch her expression change and I know it's bad news. I look into her eyes. Why did I have to look into her eyes? Her blue eyes are now a deep, dark black. I read terror in the darkness. She looks past me at an empty space and tells me that Monday is the first day of the hearing. Today is Tuesday so I've got just under a week to go before I face the man who ruled my life.

I am Candice Derman. I am angry. My numbness has been replaced with an 'I don't give a shit' attitude. Let me face this man who fucked up my life, the man I loved and who treated me like his bitch. I was the dog, and he was my master. I wagged my tail and forgave him over and over again, always thinking that tomorrow would be different. But I was stupid because nothing changed. Every day my master would come back for more and every day I would forgive him and wag my pathetic tail. I am strong-willed, opinionated, confident, noisy, playful and cocky and I let him do this to me. I said nothing. I let him hurt me, I let him ruin my future.

So now it is my time to face him in court and I will be strong. But who am I kidding? I should know that with each passing day come different moods, emotions, needs and weaknesses. With all these conflicting emotions, I need to find clarity in my life, so I've started a new trick, controlling my food intake, and this makes me feel better. Less food equals more strength.

The court date arrives. I'm sitting on a bench outside the courtroom, my legs dangling and swinging, not out of joy but out of shortness. The numbness has set in again and it overrides my fear. My mom sits close by me but I don't really care, she could be across the universe as far as I am concerned.

People walk past, some in a hurry, others as slow as snails. They all have somewhere to go; none of them wants to be here. Criminals and victims, all in chronic pain, all misunderstood.

I am in my school uniform, hair back, fresh-faced. I look neat. Maybe if I unravelled myself and they saw my true feelings, they would blame me. I sit still, neat and tidy.

I see Dad from the corner of my eye. I feel the lost years of my life well up inside me, years of him fucking me, years of pain, of joy, of lies and deceit, of loving him, of loving him, of loving him.

My numbness scale is dipping and my heart beats faster.

I am vulnerable. I am terrified. Lost. Alone. Isolated.

I've already been given a sentence, placed in an invisible jail, one I'm afraid I will never escape. A jail of guilt, self-loathing and little food.

I feel bleak. Dad's looking good, he's lost his belly. Comfortable. Strong. My anger scale rises. I could bash his confidence right out of him. How do some people remain so calm when they have committed unthinkable crimes? Can't he see that my mom and I are puppets and have lost our way? We are motionless. Our strings have been cut. We are up for sale, going pretty cheap, we need a new puppet master, someone who will lead us into the light.

The buzz from lack of food kicks in, or maybe it's a phone call from G-d to remind me, in this building, outside this courtroom, next to my mother, that I need to create my own future and demand my own sanity. My mom let someone else be the master of her ceremony and look where it got us. I need to be my own puppeteer.

I like this feeling. I don't care if it dissolves into nothingness, I'll remember the taste of my own power. Dad looks over at me and I look away. Even with this new feeling I'm not strong enough to face him now, not today, not tomorrow, not ever.

The court date is postponed. We walk into the daylight, the sun is shining and I know I have become master of Candice's ceremony.

Mom drops me off at school. 'Love you, Mom.'

'Love you, Candice.' I get out of the car.

I do love my mom and even though we are lost in this abyss, she still knows how to tug at my heartstrings.

I am going to have to be patient. I can't own my own life at fourteen. I still have to go to school, live at home and do my homework, but somehow, some way, some day, my life will be mine.

STILL FOURTEEN

Things I have to get through before I become my own boss:
1. *School.*
2. *Court.*
3. *Being a teenager.*

These are big things, but I'm up for the challenge and I see G-d smiling at me.

Summer arrives. I love the long warm days in Johannesburg, with clear blue skies and afternoon thunderstorms. In one day the weather can have many moods, and I'm no different. It is calming to know that I'm one with this earth and that I'm as fluid and changing as G-d intended.

fifteen

I am trying to get used to life without Dad, with a mom who is so hurt she is vacant and sisters who are just trying to get on with their lives. This isn't easy for me. I want attention, I want love and I want to be looked after. I decide it's time to meet my real dad. So much for being my own master of ceremonies.

The meeting of father and daughter goes like this.

'Hello, it's good to see you,' he's struggling to connect with me.

He has curly grey hair, a beard, olive green eyes, and a lined face. He is short and lean. I recognise him. I see our physical similarities but I can't get into his soul and he can't get into mine.

We talk, but our conversation is stilted. The silence echoes and I can see this is not the place I am going to get attention in the way I need and the way I want.

He is afraid to hug me. He looks at me as an abused girl and I feel nameless, a feeling I'm starting to understand well. I promise to keep in touch with him, this man, my real father.

Life becomes a series of mind-numbing events full of holes, hurt and dirt. I feel littered by it all. Mommy has lost all her money, her assets, her sanity, but luckily not her looks. Her looks need to be maintained or she could end up like Humpty Dumpty and never be put back together again. She had signed surety for Dad – Joe, I mean. He owned everything and fucked everything, excuse the pun, so Mommy doesn't have her high-flying life anymore. She's been screwed out of money and her daughter has been screwed. Period.

Mommy has to sell the house, the Porsche, the boats, the cottage at the Vaal, her antiques and her jewellery. She declares herself insolvent and begins her anorexic life.

Our house starts to stink of sadness. The cats are weeing on the furniture and I imagine that they are marking their territory in case someone comes along to take their most loved possessions away. The paintings have gone from the walls, leaving only outlines of where they once hung. The only thing hanging in their place is emptiness.

I start sleeping in my mom's bed; I am not sure why. I find no comfort next to her, but the thought of being alone in my room is unwelcome. There is no reason for anything; I am just being, surviving.

Anna left a long time ago and Lizzy is the last other mother standing. Lucas has gone and the garden has died. Gran left with Joe: blood is thicker than water, they say, or maybe it was Jesus who advised her to leave. We don't hear from my stepbrothers again; they have vanished.

My new life is horrible. I am staring into nothing-ness. I can't help wondering if living with the abuse was better than living this shipwreck of a life. I am alone, my house is empty, but my head is cluttered.

Boys keep me busy and I am in and out of rela-tionships. I'm addicted to feeling good, but it doesn't last long. I like the first moments of meeting, catch-ing a boy's eye and looking away. I enjoy the teasing and the flirting. I love the first kiss: how tongues talk to each other, the warmth, and how the wet makes me excited. But as soon as we separate and I look into their eyes, I feel a terrible sense of gloom and my next move is out the door, my next conversation is to break up with them. They must all think I'm awful but they're not the answer, they're not the cure to my disease. I don't want to have sex with anyone; my va-gina is closed for business.

I audition for a drama place at the School of the Arts. As my tragic monologue I use one of the letters a teenage girl has written to Judy Blume about her abuse. Her story is not dissimilar to mine and I shine in my delivery of living this girl's tragic life. My tears fall as I speak her words.

A voice from the adjudication panel, 'Candice, that was very believable.'

If only they knew that I am a mirror of that girl I do not know.

I pray I get into the School of the Arts; I need a ray of light in this darkness. I'm starting to collect fear like tumbleweed collects dust. Everything has been moving so slowly, days are long and nights are never-ending. I live my life thinking it's a nightmare and I wake up from sleep hoping it was. Dreams are filled with me running away from Dad, having sex with strangers, and old women cackling at me. The cackling is the worst. They have never left me, those cold, spiteful women. My life feels like the aftermath of war. The bomb has hit, the devastation is evident and no one is there to help. I am struggling to heal my internal wound. No one can see the bleeding; no one is my witness.

The only excitement I have to latch on to is that I get into the School of the Arts to study drama. I'll be an actress by day and a victim by night. My friends know nothing about my life; they don't know the tears that are shed in my mansion that is for sale. My foundation is crumbling and I'm all smiles.

Wendywood High School will soon be a memory, and Dale will be part of a past I have shut away. I have failed standard seven twice and don't know if the School of the Arts will put me through to standard eight. My report card is bad and I fail almost everything. Lack of concentration, lack of care, plain stupidity or maybe fucking chronic abuse, but nobody asks questions. I'm just a stupid, short girl with a pretty face and curls that bounce with glee. My ass happily sways and my round breasts are growing by the day. They desire a boy's touch, they show off in my T-shirt and wish to celebrate. I am their enemy, I hate them, I hate them for growing, I hate them for jiggling as I walk.

I'm trying not to eat a lot. Maybe at some stage I'll just eat an apple a day – after all, it does keep the doctor away.

My daily diet:

1. *2 x Pro-Vita.*
2. *A small slab of cheese.*
3. *1 x apple.*
4. *Salad with chicken.*

My life makes me want to be thin, to disappear.

The court date looms. Too soon it will be here, too soon I will see my dad, stand in the dock and talk of his doings. I will smell his smoky hands and try to hold on to the anger, locking away my vulnerability that I wear like an invisible cloak. I will not shed tears that fall in the dark.

I am in trouble. My heart is broken and I am still walking. Dead.

My first experience at the School of the Arts is great: a new school and a fresh start. Mom speaks to the headmaster and tells him of our woes. The good man puts me up to standard eight even though I failed standard seven dismally, but someone has to give me a break. If failing standard seven twice is a talent, then going into standard eight clueless turns my talent into a performance. No struggling. I'll force myself to be academic, to be popular, to be talented. I'm ready to unveil the new me.

I'm sitting in a circle on the floor with the other students. Our drama teacher tells us that we have to introduce ourselves and talk a bit about our lives. One of the students starts speaking, and I start daydreaming about the Candice that could have been me.

I imagine a young girl living with her mom, dad and four sisters, a girl with a life full of joy. I imagine a life where laughter is her first language, where her dad is a kind king and her mom a beautiful queen. A home where darkness and pain are illegal and her childhood is filled with love and the possibilities of life's magic.

'Candice, it's your turn.'

I introduce myself to the class. I'm an actress and I do it well.

'I'm Candice Derman,' I smile.

The class watches and I put on the show of a lifetime. I lie about my life. What else am I to do?

I've always lied about the skeletons in my closet. They're not for others to know about. I talk about my passion for acting. This is a truth and I gleam with confidence.

Even I believe my performance and start feeling good: this is going to be a new chapter for me and I will be happy. My lies can be kind when I mean no harm; they make me believe everything will be okay.

FIFTEEN

My real dad is not around, which is neither here nor there. Our relationship is murky and I realise he cannot save me. I'm back to being my own master of ceremonies, and I am feeling less disappointed. What did I expect from him? Balloons? A 'Welcome Home' sign? Dusty presents he was collecting for me? Did I expect him to hold me and tell me everything would be okay, words that adults can never say?

I'm not the eight-year-old he left, and I make my own rules and decide my own destiny. I'll learn to look after myself, navigate my own way. If I don't, I will drown in my sorrows, slit my wrists or take tablets. The unease with my dad, the unease with my mom and the dislike of myself are so frustrating but I have to keep going, keep struggling to free myself.

Another date in court. Another postponement. Another date in court.

I see Joe, he sees me. I still dare not look. We're at a restaurant near the court and he is sitting at a table across from my mom and me. If I don't laugh at the situation I'll cry forever, so I force myself to laugh. I'm laughing at the horror, I'm laughing at my fear. For the occasion I order a toasted cheese sandwich, with extra fat on my ass, but I'm deserving of this banquet under the circumstances. The toasted cheese goes down my throat like thick tar, each swallow forced. I will enjoy this toastie.

I leave empty-handed. No prizes, no hearing, just a weary heart, heavy thighs and a full stomach. Soon his day will come.

Things I love at fifteen:

1. *Acting.*
2. *The School of the Arts.*
3. *My drama teacher.*
4. *Poetry.*
5. *Apples (they're about the only thing I want to eat).*

Things I hate at fifteen:

1. *Joe.*
2. *Court days.*
3. *Academic subjects.*
4. *Food (apples excluded).*
5. *Night-time.*

sixteen

Thank goodness for drama and for a school that celebrates my sixteen-year-old talent. I'm in my new world of Sophocles' Greek tragedies, Shakespeare and D.H. Lawrence. These men knew about the broken mystery and magic of life, and I am in love. So many poems to learn, plays to read and productions to act in. I'm making many friends. I even confide in some and they are kind with my secrets and hold them close.

My drama teacher, Mr Davidson, is wonderful. He believes in my talent and injects me with a spark of life. I feel fuelled with excitement to perform in my first major production. It's *The House of Bernardo. Alba* by Federico Garcia Lorca, and I play Adela. She is a carefree, loving girl who is in love with her sister's fiancé. They make love outdoors and celebrate their love secretly, but the family finds out and this wreaks devastation. At the end of the play Adela hangs herself. What a way to heal myself. Every night Candice Derman hangs herself only to live again. I feel the pain. The desperation. The end. Adela heals me and I kill her.

I flourish in my new environment. My school marks are still bad, but I've got a talent, a place to hide, and nothing can bring me down.

I've been dating a boy called Brett, who is kind, gentle, patient and intelligent. He was in Dale's class at Wendywood High School. We kept in touch and kept getting closer. His kindness has made me want to tell him about what Joe did to me. With my heart thumping in my head I begin telling my new boy-friend.

'My stepdad abused me.'

Brett's eyes are wide and gentle, allowing me to carry on.

'It started when I was eight. At first it began with him touching me and then he raped me when I was eleven. It carried on until I was nearly fifteen.'

Head thumping, heart thumping, they are one in-strument.

'I'm sorry,' Brett moves his hands to my face, looks me in the eyes, 'you didn't deserve for anything bad to happen to you.'

I begin to cry, huge drops leave my eyes, the tears just keep falling, they are uncontrollable. It feels so good to cry in a boy's gentle embrace. Brett is silent for a long time and allows my years of pain to cry out of me. After my rainstorm, I'll be dehydrated.

'Thank you,' I say through tears and snot, my eyes red.

After that day with Brett I begin to feel stronger; a burden has been lifted from my shoulders. I am still in the wilderness, but I don't feel that there is a lion constantly gnawing at my leg. I'm still not into mating season: sex scares me, and although I enjoy the foreplay, I can't do the final act. Brett offers me constant round-the-clock love, but I feel frustrated at my inability to take our relationship further, and my heart no longer wants to be with him.

'I'm sorry, I can't be with you.' Another break-up. Bad habits are hard to kick.

'Why Candice? I don't get it, it's so good between us.'

'It's not you, it's me.'

This he will believe, after all I am the complicated one.

'I'm sorry, so sorry, I just need to sort myself out. I love you, but I'm not good at always loving me.'

And with those words, Brett and Candice are over. I don't have to revisit my sexual issues for a while. I'm grateful to Brett for sharing in my burden. Telling someone who cares helps me unload my rucksack. It's as if they carry away a small part of me, and I don't have to be all of me alone. One day my rucksack will be empty, I will share my story with the people I love, and I will slowly heal. But not anytime soon.

Something's gone missing in Mommy. Her electric blue eyes have turned a permanent deep, dark blue. Her shine has gone and even her mask can't hide her pain. She is in a constant state of shock. Mommy's shock is loud; it's talking to all her friends, or even strangers if they are kind enough to offer her an ear. She yaps about what has happened and they listen with foaming mouths, loving the saga of Joe and his little women. I wish she would just keep her mouth shut: she exposes me, I'm Exhibit A, a prop, a big part of the story, maybe even the lead.

Tight-lipped I ask, 'Mom, are you okay?'

Of course she is not okay, but I've got to say something. Even in my 'I hate you' mode, I still care.

She answers, 'I don't know how I am going to cope with everything. I don't have money, I don't know where we are going to live or what's going to happen to us.'

I offer no comfort. I don't know how she'll get money but I do know that my mom has a way of getting help at the eleventh hour, then all her worries go under the carpet for a short time, a very short time. She's a woman greedy for help.

My mom's friends don't seem to be good therapists; she's not getting the answers she wants from them, so she finds a new way, a new path of 'future knowledge enlightenment'.

'Joe is evil, he's a psychopath. I'm going to remarry. I have a choice of two men, one younger, one older, both European.'

My mom has just been to a fortune teller and she's ranting and raving. Since the madness of our lives began, my mom has found some kind of solace in people telling her about her future. She's been to four fortune tellers and none of them brings her peace. She seems possessed after she sees them. I watch her pacing, her sad blue eyes on stalks.

She goes on and on ...

Shit, I want out, away from here, away from her, away from this life.

But I soften when she tells me that the fortune teller told her I'm going to be a famous actress. This I want to hear, this I like a lot. Maybe the fortune teller is right after all. My mood lifts. I don't want out, I want to eat, maybe a bagel with cream cheese or a blueberry muffin. The delights of life, the change of moods, the opportunities, the choices.

I am a very confused teenager, and anger can arrive and depart in seconds. Sadness changes to happiness, hope to failure. I'm in and out of 'Oh shit, I want to die', and 'Lucky me, I want to live', and right now I want to live, live to be that famous actress.

'Mom, can we go and get a muffin?'

She too is in a good mood: after all, her prince in shining armour is going to save her and take her away from her debilitating pain.

The truth is I'm fucked. I want to throw up the blueberry muffin; I don't deserve scrumptious food. I'm a victim of abuse and my mom is hurt, alone and petrified.

'Yes, I'd love one.' And off we go, packaged so neatly, mother and daughter.

We don't eat home-cooked meals anymore: Joe took that away from us. We can't sit like a family and play happy; it's all gone too far. So every night we eat takeaways. I'm into haloumi cheese salad and

I've cut out bread, which seems to be working. My thighs are shrinking, so a bit of haloumi cheese can't hurt me.

'What do you want for dinner, Cands?'

'Haloumi salad.' Again and again I want to eat haloumi salad.

Out of the blue I've noticed my mom's energy changing again. Her lipstick is a lighter shade of pink, her eyes have their old shine back and there is a 'tra-la-la' in her step. I wonder what it could be, what could be making my mother happy again. And then she tells me. She's started dating a man. I'm thinking, 'No fucking way. How can you let a man into our lives after everything we've been through?'

'I'm going out with him tonight.'

'That's nice,' I say through my gritted teeth.

'Cands, you're going to love him.'

But I won't, I'll hate him. I'll hate him because I already know him. He will be dark with brown eyes and dark hair, Portuguese, Italian or Greek, some continental fuck who seduces my mom and makes her feel good, too good, the lie good.

At sixteen I've learned about the lie good.

Examples of the lie good:

1.   *When a boy I don't care about tells me I'm sexy, I feel good, but it's fleeting and soon I'll feel like my chubby self again.*

2.   *When a boy I don't care about kisses me, I feel all*
     giddy and excited, but as soon as he stops I feel
     guilty, bad and once again back to my chubby self.

So that's the lie good and I've learned I have to find
the truth good: the good that's good just because it's
good. Brett was the truth good but he wasn't the one
for me.

I'm watching my mom's excitement, all her desire
wrapped up in this man. This Giovanni, the new man
I now hate.

Things move quickly. Mommy sells our house, as
she needs the cash. When money goes, it goes fast.
We move five minutes away from the house of Joe
into a small, pretty house, but with this house comes
Giovanni, and the pretty disappears in my eyes.

I have lost:

1.   *Dad.*
2.   *Dale.*
3.   *My mom.*

It feels like Mom has gone far, far away. We don't speak
the same language anymore, we are from different parts
of the world. I'm angry with her for everything, even
though she never meant for any of this evil to happen. I
have a burning in my heart and her new man brings out
a rage in me, a war in my world. I openly refuse to be
a part of my mom and Giovanni's team. I don't eat his

food, which is easy to do considering I prefer a don't-eat buffet in any case. I won't talk to him, acknowledge him or look at him. I pretend he is not here and I am a ghost in my own house.

'Candice, why can't you be nice to Giovanni? He's in my life and you have to accept it.'

My mom doesn't know that I don't have to accept anything. Joe gave me an internal angry tool and I know how to use it.

'I hate him, I'll never accept him and you can't make me.'

What more is there to say? I'm sixteen, in the 'comfort' of my teenage years, I have my period and I'm pissed off, so pissed off I am about to explode and splatter angry body parts all over my mother's floor.

Somehow the prosecutor has managed to get me off having to stand in the dock and face Joe, to tell everyone how he unhooked my bra a million times and knew the ins and outs of my youthful vagina.

The psychologist and prosecutor will talk for me, and they believe it will be enough to put him behind bars. I have mixed feelings. I am relieved, but there is a part of me that wanted to face Joe, to tell him how much he hurt me, make him face my damaged goods. But this is not to be. So no more court dates, no more court buildings and no more seeing Joe. I just have to wait and see what the judge decides.

My life seems to have been one big build-up, fol-lowed by an explosion, and now silence is the end result. All my anxiety and all my stress are in a puddle under me. I know it's a good thing that I didn't talk on behalf of the broken me, but my lingering worry is that I'll have to carry this with me forever.

For now I will sleep, a peaceful sleep, a sleep that I lost out on growing up because Joe kept prodding me every night. For now I will put this feeling away, maybe never to be revisited.

Mom's moved on with her life, hurt, bruised but intact. Romy and her rucksack are overseas, and she is driving a tractor on a kibbutz in Israel. This is really a man's job but if a girl's in pain, manual labour is a good antidepressant. She left as soon as she finished school; I don't think she could look our life in the eye. I don't blame her: if I were old enough, I would run as far away as I could.

Jodi is on her way to being a big shot in advertising, climbing the ranks fast and furiously. Perfect for a young woman running away from the shackles of a hurt family. She is afraid of chaos and wants balance; moving out is the best way to move forward. Kim's living in Durban and working as a personal trainer, eating chicken and rice and perfecting her already perfect body. Outward perfection never shows the scars of a past; what a perfect way to show the world you're one up on it. She has a boyfriend, has created a new truth and is doing well, considering.

So my lovely life at home is just Mommy and Giovanni. Daily fights with him because my 'I don't see

Giovanni' technique isn't working. I bombed with that one.

'I hate you!' Tears streaming down my face, doors slamming.

My only option is to move in with my real dad.

'I'm moving out.'

'Fine, but don't ever come back to this house again,' my mom retorts with her clenched jaw.

'I'll never come back. I hate what you've done to our lives. I hate the way you need men.'

More tears, more slamming doors, uncontrollable anger, rage.

Things I'm angry about:

1. *Everything.*

I pack my short life into suitcases and boxes, and put my heart away. Scared of nothing, scared of everything, I move in with my real dad. He tries to discipline me but I'm not having a father who hasn't raised me telling me what to do. He can use his father skills on my toddler stepsister.

I'm disruptive, I feel out of place, I'm hurt and he can't fill the emptiness in me. Living with him is no place for a post-abuse teenager. My dad and step-mom struggle to understand me and I struggle to understand them. My bedroom only has space for a mattress and there is nowhere for me to hide my constantly falling tears. They fight a lot and I know I'm the cause of their arguments. They get strange calls at all hours of the night telling my dad to castrate Joe, shouting at him for doing nothing. This sets a tone of unease in this fragile family home.

My list of how I think my dad should be looking after me:

1. *Show he cares.*
2. *Be loving.*
3. *Tell me he's so sorry that I was hurt.*
4. *Create meaningful moments.*
5. *Take me to the movies.*
6. *Give me a bigger bedroom.*

I'm naughty at school, naughty at home and I'm in trouble a lot. Maybe I like the attention, maybe I like not being liked. I do know I don't like living with my dad. He has his new family and I'm not part of that. I'm his daughter from the other side of the tracks, the black sheep, the unwashed, the used.

Another option opens up: become a weekly boarder at the School of the Arts. I am so excited to be away from both my parents, those adults who don't understand me, adults who look at me with pain in their eyes.

So boarding school here I come.

still sixteen

I'm enjoying boarding school, even the rules and regulations. I like the school bell that acts as a strict parent. I like having no eyes on me: no vulnerable mother looking at me with guilt and sadness, no strict father trying to raise this grown-up me.

This is my new daily routine, without chaos, secrets or Joe's shadow over me:

06:30   Wake-up bell. Shower. Get dressed. Make bed. Clean room. Room inspection.

07:30   Breakfast.

08:00   Walk to class.

12:00   Dining hall. Eat lunch. Socialise with friends.

13:00   Back to class.

14:30   Home bell. Back to my room. Off with my uniform. On with my casuals.

15:00   Homework bell. Out with my books. Thinking cap on.

16:30   Teatime.

18:30   Dining hall. Eat dinner. Socialise with friends.

19:30   Drama rehearsals. Perform.

21:00   Finish rehearsals.

21:30   Back to my room. Communal shower. Pyjamas on. Get ready for bed.

22:00   Lights-out time, or not. Some rules are meant to be broken.

After the lights go out, my friends and I sneak into one of the bedrooms and chat about all things drama and gossip.

I'm trying hard at school. I'm still behind academically, but I'm pushing myself to study and understand concepts that don't matter to me. I'm really a part of something and I'm loving my life, loving my friends. My moments of fear only visit for short intervals, because I am too busy being the happy me.

I stay with my mom at weekends and it's going well. We are still unstitched but getting on. My burning anger is not as fiery anymore and only a small flame still flickers. I love my mom and I don't want a life without her.

At last things are going well. I am trying hard to be clever, succeeding at being nice and working to forget my unfitting past. I truly want to succeed at being me.

I am sixteen and filled with the wisdom of life.

My wisdom list:

1.   *Make the right choices.*
2.   *A man cannot take away a woman's pain.*

3. *Sweets make you fat. Don't eat crap.*
4. *Adults don't have the answers.*

I'm in drama class when my name is called out over the intercom. I go to reception and see one of Mommy's friends (or not?). She used to date Joe and somehow became a part of our lives, which I'm happy about because I like her.

'Hi, Candice.'

'Hi, Cecile.'

'Let's go into the playground and talk. I have something to tell you.'

I inhale. I use my skill of holding my breath, afraid of what may happen if I exhale. We walk through my creative, beautiful school past one hall with ballet dancers who perform the most graceful moves and another with musicians playing sweet, melodic music.

Cecile and I walk past all this creative hope into the green and blue day, grass so very green and sky so very blue. No music, no dancers, just Cecile, some tweeting, happy birds and me. We walk and don't talk, our shoes swish through the grass. Cecile stops. I stop. She talks.

'Joe has been sentenced to two years in jail, and may only serve six months with good behaviour.'

The tweeting of the birds fills my ears. I didn't want to hear that. I wanted to enjoy the hope of this day, hold onto the beauty of Johannesburg, hold onto moving forward and living a good life. The birds stop tweeting but Cecile's still talking.

'Your mom's a wreck and I thought it was best that I came to tell you about Joe. I know this must be so hard for you.'

Cecile's now hugging my frigid body.

I'm not sure how to respond; I don't know how I'm feeling.

Joe tried to break my spirit, he made me grow up too quickly. I'm not a virgin, I'll never have a first because Joe was my first. Oh my G-d … that thought hits me and tears come tumbling down. This man who broke my family, who made us unstable, who taught us fear, only gets two years. This man who violated me on every level only gets two years and I, Candice Derman, am sentenced to a lifetime of being a victim, of being a child of abuse. Oh my G-d, oh my G-d, I am never going to be normal. I will always carry Joe in my veins, he will always walk through my thoughts and crush my hopes of a normal, happy life.

I can't hug Cecile back; my body won't accept comfort in another one of my broken life moments.

Cecile lets go of me and just stares at me. What can she say? What can she do?

'I'm sorry, Candice.'

'Yah, me too.' My secret weapon has taken over; numbness knows my body so well, it infiltrates all of me. Joe still has the power to make my life's colour fade to black in an instant.

I go back to class, detached. We're playing trust games. You have to close your eyes, fall backwards and let the other person catch you.

My checklist of an abused girl:

1. *Fear. Tick*
2. *Panic. Tick*
3. *Weight loss (thank G-d). Tick*
4. *Confusion. Tick*
5. *Lack of concentration. Tick*
6. *Moodiness. Tick*
7. *Self-doubt. Tick*
8. *Suicidal thoughts. Tick*

Life is so difficult. The moon is full and I see no beauty in that. I cannot connect the dots and sort out my life. I can't spell, add or subtract. I hate geography, I don't care about stalactites and stalagmites. I am distracted and restless. My tummy rumbles with hunger and sadness, it rumbles because I ignore it. I am a skeleton of a person. My mind is scrambled, a messy ramble in my head. I'm a little girl lost, but physically I am positively glowing. I win Miss Empire, boarding school beauty queen, and now I'm wearing yet another sash. I want to stop being so up and down; I want my heart to stop racing and learn to beat regularly.

My sixteen-year-old life is so confusing, even more than is usual. A big part of my struggle is the normality of my life. Sometimes I feel good, have a sense of being lucky to be alive, to see a full moon with eyes that aren't blind to its beauty, to eat fresh fruit, watch a good movie, lie in a bubble bath, chew bubblegum and put mascara on my lashes.

I like feeling good, good about myself. I want the sunshine, the calm, I want a mother and not a friend, a father and not a lover, I want a boyfriend. I'd like to share my life with a person who's bright, who wants to play and laugh, live in a world where we travel our own path, create our own happiness, and more than anything else I want to see myself happy. My greed for a good life is insatiable.

I pass standard eight. My marks are low but good enough to get me through to standard nine. People tell me I should work harder and I'm thinking, 'You have no idea how fucking well I've done.' Just a few more years to go and I'm out of school, footloose and fancy-free. I need to learn to stay afloat. This may be a lifetime of work. I'm sixteen and I have a long road to travel.

Things I learned from my mom:

1. *Never open up to strangers.*
2. *Avoid bad boys.*
3. *Don't let a man control you.*
4. *Don't rely only on others.*
5. *Trust very few people.*

Things I learned from Joe:

1. *Fear.*
2. *Guilt.*
3. *Insecurity.*
4. *What it feels like to be an object.*
5. *How to fly above myself.*

My two greatest influences growing up taught me many things, but the things that I have to teach myself will heal me the most:

1. *Never be a victim.*
2. *Be strong in my head even if my body isn't.*
3. *Love hard and have meaningful relationships.*
4. *Play in the moment and be grateful for every day.*
5. *Believe deep down that I deserve good things.*

epilogue

Abuse is like an unnatural disaster: everything that is lost must be rebuilt, and I have had to rebuild all of me.

After Joe went to jail I struggled to see in colour. I floated in and out of numbness, sadness and happiness. I believed that I was talented, special, attractive and invisible, untalented and unattractive. Food became my secret. Some months I'd eat almost nothing and during others I'd consume the entire contents of my fridge. Having this control over myself, and using it in ways that no one knew about, made me feel stronger.

Romy visited from time to time and we would watch soapies and sleep together in spoons. I passed matric, got an acting agent and started waitressing. I moved back to live with my mom and stayed until I was twenty-five. At times we walked hand in hand and at other times we lived in separate universes. I carried her pain as if it were my own. I wanted to bandage her wounds and take away her past. But I couldn't. So I tried to heal my own pain, bandage my own wounds and leave the past behind.

I loved some men with everything I had, enjoyed and hated my sexuality and found solace in being complicated. I walked into walls and made mistakes so that I could feel something.

I carried my abuse with me because I didn't know where else I could put it. It burned like acid and pain would come to me from the shadows. Joe never visited me in my nightmares; he stopped being a person and became a cancer. He became my very own private illness.

I succeeded as an actress in South Africa, but realised that hiding behind my characters didn't make me happy. I acted to forget but my body wanted me to remember, and carrying my secret diminished me.

A month after my twenty-fifth birthday, I met and married my perfect man. He asked me to be his wife after only two days; I said yes and we eloped. That was nearly nineteen years ago. I have been blessed to find my lifetime friend, a man who pushes me to be brave, never feels sorry for me and sees my sunshine when I don't see any.

For the first few years of our marriage, when I wasn't dancing with happiness, I cried about my past. I dabbled in an eating disorder but became bored with not looking after the body that had worked so hard to protect me. I taught myself to eat with love and look after the physical me.

I faced good and bad, and both welcomed me. I wasn't able to run away from the bad, so I learned to accept it, and that forced me to love the good harder.

I told Jonathan that only I could heal my pain. I was right. Eventually I stopped crying for the child in me and embraced her, and we became a team. She lives with me every day now and has helped me to remain childlike.

I started writing this book because I always knew that I needed to find answers for myself. I began healing a long, long time ago: the very first moment after Joe touched me. That day my body taught me how to survive, taught me how to use my imagination. It has taken me on journeys far away; my dreams have made a beautiful life possible, and my love for kittens, birthdays and the afternoon thunderstorms of Johannesburg saved me. These are the things that helped me to remain a child, to remain Candice Derman.

As I have grown older, my abuse has become less and less a part of me. I don't know how it happened, how one day the storm began to settle, but it did. Maybe it was G-d, maybe it was my desire to heal, and maybe it was because I was born with a gift to love and to love without fear. I think it must be all of these things.

I don't think of myself as a wounded woman with a painful past. I am a woman who is so lucky to have understood kind love in amongst the bad from such an early age. I am a wife not a survivor, I am a woman not a victim, I am a person who will continue to ask questions like a child but who will hopefully find answers as an adult.

My mom, sisters and I are pieces of the same jigsaw puzzle strewn across the world. We don't all fit together perfectly anymore and I am closer to some of them than others. Over the years we have spoken about Joe and the chaos he caused. Sometimes a cloud still hangs over us and the rain falls, but we have all moved forward in life, created our own families and made new histories for ourselves. Our surnames are all different, but we remain blood sisters. Memories endure of picnics and five girls in a Volkswagen with the best mother in the world. We know we can't fix what has been broken but we can love the innocence of life before Joe.

Time can be kind, ticking clocks move forward and I'm the furthest I have been from my childhood story, both physically and mentally.

London is my home and there are no parts of me on the pavements, in the playground or inside a Wendy house. I have become a mother and the human wonder that made my belly grow into its soft femaleness has changed me. Summer was made out of love, that is where her story began and a new chapter of mine emerged.

My question has an answer. I was abused and I no longer search for the parts of me that were stolen. Summer is not being raised in the shadow of my girlhood, instead we search for fairies in secret places and dance in tutus. We are princesses, superheroes, explorers, architects and storytellers. There are footprints behind me, but alongside are my husband

and daughter as I walk in the bright light of the present. I'm greedy to enjoy life and grateful I can.

My journey continues, but this is what I know for sure:

1. *I live a good life and am stronger than I ever could have imagined.*
2. *I love my husband and daughter more than I hated Joe.*

My name is Candice Derman. I am short with curly, dark hair, blue eyes, and olive skin. Joe has faded and I can see in colour again.